THE CO-DESIGN CANVAS

A proven design tool for societal impact

Wina Smeenk

BIS Publishers

Table of contents

Preface

Congratulations! You have decided to
join forces in tackling a societal challenge.
Good for you!

The Co-Design Canvas can help you. It is a tool that facilitates open, transparent dialogue about everyone's experiences and interests, the alignment of expectations and goals, the creation of understanding and insights, and the exchange of knowledge, positions, power relationships and shared responsibilities in the planning, execution and assessment of a co-design process.

You can, of course, start reading this book from the very beginning with the Introduction and learn more about the background of the Co-Design Canvas. Or you can launch directly into the nitty-gritty by reading the Co-Design Canvas Manual in Chapter 4. Alternatively, perhaps you might first like to hear about how others have used the Canvas? If so, start with Chapter 5. Clearly, whatever your preference, it is completely up to you how you read this book!

1

○○○ ○○
○○○ ○○
     ○○
     ○○

Introduction

Our world has reached a tipping point. Societal challenges have become increasingly pressing. They affect us all: politicians, citizens, government officials, business professionals, NGOs, designers and researchers. Truly understanding and tackling them is difficult, because no single stakeholder or organisation is wholly responsible for them, and everything is connected, interwoven and in a current state of flux and change. Moreover, there is mutual interaction, involvement and entanglements between people, non-humans and technology.

Systemic challenges that are based on the relationships, interactions and experiences of stakeholders and their environments are dynamic. They evolve. And this can make it difficult to even see the playing field. Challenges then become orphaned and stakeholders unable, or unwilling, to make all kinds of important decisions. This ambiguity leads to a lot of uncertainty. When combined with blind spots, implicit world views, tacit mechanisms and latent values, this also hinders change and limits social innovation capacity. Which raises the following question.

How, as a stakeholder, can you gain agency to act on these complex challenges in a way that adds value to the collective?

The substantial number of grand societal challenges around us demand new approaches to collectively build alternative sustainable futures. Nowadays design, and more specifically co-design, is increasingly seen as a potential approach for guiding people, teams, organisations and coalitions towards change, transformation and transition. Since design can deal with uncertainty and is both optimistic and inquisitive in nature. Design can imagine what does not yet exist and it can envision, depict and visualise the unknown. As such, it is particularly well suited in imagining alternative futures.

Whereas these so-called co-design processes are becoming more mainstream, many movers and shakers in multi-stakeholder coalitions lack practical guidance. Although scholars and practitioners offer several co-design methodologies and methods, there does not seem to be an instrument that goes beyond these methods and supports new coalitions with an overview of a co-design process. One that will help them make shared and fundamental co-design decisions. This begs the next key question.

How can we create a co-design culture, approach and structure that will encourage stakeholders to open up and reveal their implicit world views, interests, knowledge and power, or lack thereof? One that will support their agency and provides more inclusive, radical and shared opportunities for change.

This requires a tool that explains what co-design entails, supports new coalitions with an overview of an emerging co-design process that facilitates the making of shared and fundamental co-design decisions. We need a concept that everybody understands, a concept that facilitates the co-design description or definition. And we need a shared starting point and a joint language. The challenge lies in making this concept simple, relevant and intuitively understandable, but without simplifying the complexity of how systems, organisations and collaborations function.

For these reasons, this book offers the novel Co-Design Canvas and its Manual as an intermediate-level knowledge product based on an existing, theoretical framework, an empirical case study and a diversity of experiences in education and practice[1]. The Co-Design Canvas specifically identifies eight variables that influence and form the basis of a co-design process. These are: the co-design context; the purpose; the stakeholders; the concrete results; the impact; the focus; the setting; and the activities.

This practical Canvas is an easy-to-use instrument. It will help multi-stakeholder coalitions and/or their facilitators to flexibly plan, conduct and evaluate a co-design process or initiative around societal challenges with governments, citizens, businesses, NGOs, knowledge institutions and other stakeholders. The Canvas can offer a coalition a joint language in the way it describes, explores and works on co-design for societal challenges and creates alternative futures through iterative pathways and parallel activities. Moreover, in addition to getting coalitions to discuss the problematic context, a common purpose, desired positive impact, concrete results, stakeholders' interests, experiences and knowledge, the Canvas also encourages stakeholders to acknowledge their level of, or lack of, power. This is something that is not often done in design. The latter can create trust, a more equal level playing field, empathy, and help manage expectations, all of which are greatly needed in overcoming today's grand societal challenges. Moreover, the Canvas ensures that everyone's voice is truly heard. At the end of the day, the Canvas and its Manual will help people to find common ground and literally, read off the same page.

'literally, read off the same page'

This book has been organised into seven chapters. In Chapter 2, I will give an overview of how co-design can help to tackle societal challenges. Then in Chapter 3, I will explain how the Canvas came about and how it can support you and your co-working partners. Then, in Chapter 4 the Co-Design Canvas and its Manual are introduced and discussed. Chapter 5 is about the Co-Design Canvas in the wild, so to speak, in the real world. Brought to life by five double interviews, this chapter illustrates how the Canvas has been used by people of various backgrounds in several places during the past two years. We have concluded the book with an epilogue, acknowledgements, references and weblinks.

---

1   A knowledge product is defined as the form in which knowledge is disclosed to others, such as in papers, intermediate-level knowledge forms, or other tools. In Van Turnhout, K., Andriessen, D., Cremers, P.H.M. (Eds), (2023). Handboek Ontwerp gericht Wetenschappelijk Onderzoek. Boom Uitgevers. Pp.23-37.

Design transforms current situations into preferred ones, whereas co-design is defined as making use of collective creativity throughout the entire collaborative design process.

Co-design can be characterised by the eight key decisions that constitute a co-design process. These eight decisions take into account the four main questions asked by a coalition: why; who; what; how? The Canvas is a blueprint for a joint-design process of different communities of practices, such as business, government, non-profit, research, education and society.

2

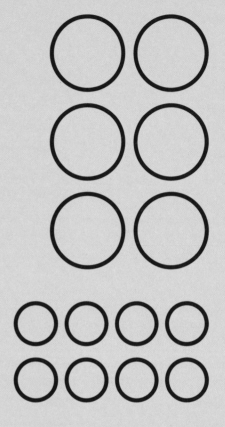

Societal challenges

Our society is going through major changes. You need look no further than current societal challenges, such as climate change, inequality, the COVID-19 crisis, and so the list goes on. Transitions in areas like energy, circularity, care, agriculture, water, food and safety are shaping our future. The increasingly visible climate crisis is forcing us to reduce our CO_2 emissions worldwide as quickly as possible, and thus mitigate the consequences of climate change. The influence of digitisation, algorithms and Artificial Intelligence (AI) as a system technology is putting pressure on political, private and public institutions, organisational forms and ways of doing things. This is increasing citizens' uncertainty and insecurity and requiring that we find new ways of organising ourselves and living together. Income disparity has increased considerably over the past few years and this is now reflected in social tensions, polarisation and reduced support for measures and changes.

In short, the Western world has reached a tipping point. Societal challenges have become increasingly pressing. They affect us all: politicians, citizens, government officials, business professionals, NGOs, designers and researchers. Truly understanding and tackling these challenges and their mechanisms is difficult, because no single stakeholder or organisation is wholly responsible for them and everything is connected, interwoven and in a current state of flux and change. And, of course, there is constant mutual interaction, entanglement and involvement between people, non-human actors and technology. Furthermore, systemic challenges that are based on the relationships, interactions and experiences between stakeholders and their environments are dynamic,

which makes challenges multi-layered and likely to evolve. All this makes it more difficult to see the playing field, obtain a collective overview and move forward together. This, in turn, makes stakeholders unable, or unwilling, to make all kinds of important (shared) decisions. Urgent societal challenges thus become stranded and orphaned between people, spheres of life, disciplines and domains.

In the wake of the industrial-, experience- and knowledge-economy eras, we are moving closer and closer towards a so-called transformation-, doughnut- or purpose-economy. For a better world, the focus is now on emotional, meaningful, ethical and sustainably produced and traded products, services and systems. One stakeholder cannot single-handedly solve the major and systemic challenges of our time. To achieve meaningful ways of thinking and positive change at a societal level, a wide variety of stakeholders from knowledge institutions, the business community, governments and society in general, need to join forces as partners in multi-value networks. Consequently, the challenges we face are not only changing in content, they are also changing in character.

The developments outlined in the first paragraph impact our society in a cultural, economic, industrial, ecological and social sense. Challenges therefore, are of an increasingly multifaceted nature. They require a multi-value creation approach in which it is no longer possible to look at a challenge from a single perspective. This not only applies to the content of challenges that require greater integration, but certainly also to the way in which those challenges are tackled.

Tackling societal challenges is not easy.
Co-design processes contain many uncertainties and variables.

Society is confronted by multiple societal challenges and crises that are high complex:
- Societal challenges are unpredictable and dynamic
- Societal challenges are multiple
- Societal challenges cannot be fully investigated
- Societal challenges have no single, conclusive solution

Our traditional linear waterfall models of problem analysis, solution design and implementation are no longer workable:
- Explanatory research aims to unravel complexity
- Research by design wants to embrace complexity
- Unite all relevant aspects in co-design processes

Coalitions crave knowledge that is actionable, that can inform action:
- Key enabling methodologies and tools need to be developed
- Intermediate level knowledge products need to be developed

Iterative work (co-design and reflection) is required to understand and tackle societal challenges:
- To find out what is going on and what needs to be taken into account
- To find out who is and who is not involved and have an interest and knowledge
- To discover whether and when something works and when it does not
- To discover why something works (mechanisms/drivers/leverage points)
- To improve local situations

The substantial number of grand societal challenges facing us call for new approaches in collectively imagining and building alternative, sustainable futures. Nowadays, design, but more specifically co-design, is increasingly seen as a possible approach for guiding people, teams, organisations and coalitions towards change, transformation and transition. Design can deal with uncertainty; it is optimistic and inquisitive in nature. Design can imagine what does not yet exist and can envision, represent and visualise the unknown. In this respect it is particularly well suited when it comes to imagining alternative futures. Supported by abductive logic that is based on the values that people aspire to and their accompanying mechanisms, design can establish leverage points, develop surprising frames and reframes and take creative leaps that can lead to radical change. As a result, design can be seen as the facilitator of fundamental societal change. What is more, a co-design and empathic approach makes it possible to identify and share stakeholders' individual differences and interests, as well as shared perspectives and ambitions. This lays the groundwork for creating new bonds - potentially new and multi-value networks - and co-imagining alternative futures.

While these so-called co-design processes are becoming more mainstream, many movers and shakers in multi-stakeholder coalitions lack practical guidance in dynamic and systemic challenges that involve entwined relationships, interactions and experiences between stakeholders and their environments. Although scholars and practitioners offer several co-design methodologies and methods, there does not seem to be an instrument that goes beyond these methods and supports new coalitions with an overview of a co-design process capable of making shared and fundamental co-design decisions. To make this co-design potential work in the complex systems that our societal challenges constitute, design itself needs to shift along with our transforming world. It is therefore itself in a state of flux. Consequently, design needs to adopt new methodological and flexible strategies that support multiple stakeholders in adaptively and empathically responding to dynamic contexts and complex collaborations. Efforts to tackle urgent societal challenges from an economic and technological perspective (culture, approach and structure) as if we still live in an industrial-, experience- or knowledge-economy, would thus be ill-advised.

The question is: how can we create a co-design culture, approach and structure that will encourage stakeholders to open up and reveal their implicit world views, interests, knowledge and power, or lack thereof? One that will support their agency and provides more inclusive, radical and shared opportunities for change. I think it is vital that designers and stakeholders become aware of the multi-value (social-cultural-ecological-economical) design decisions that lie ahead. If we are to redefine 'growth' in terms of quality of life and optimise multi-value creation in inclusive value networks, we must drastically change the way we live and work in Western society. How can we support, add to and co-realise the necessary metamorphosis? I feel that co-design will be a meaningful starting point in rethinking and reimagining societal challenges and I argue that all relevant stakeholders should be involved and responsible for this creative act.

Since we, as stakeholders, did not design our own habits and conventions - we grew up with them and accepted them as reality - we are the ones who can break them and imagine alternative futures. To do so, however, we will need an appropriate approach. To this end, all stakeholders, business professionals, NGOs, government officials, citizens, tutors, students, designers and researchers will need to let go of and reject ideas, techniques, methods, procedures and conventions that do not work and instead seek promising new avenues of thought. Surrounded by wicked challenges, as we are, it is vital that we take and develop a more systemic co-design approach. One in which stakeholders are given the space to play their respective parts, assume their responsibilities and share the benefits, and through which both the ecosystem and social complexity are appropriately navigated. In seeking an approach that goes beyond methods, one that reveals blind spots and implicit values and rethinks current conventions and structures that ultimately lead to radical societal change and impact, we need to better understand the interconnections in a societal challenge, the (implicit) values that stakeholders aspire to and the (latent) mechanisms within them.

This new approach calls for situated strategies. Due to the dynamic context and new insights obtained as the co-design process develops, stakeholders' presence and/or their respective positions can change. More importantly, it requires a transitional approach, culture and structure (Rotmans & Loorbach, 2009) that goes beyond methods (Woolrych, 2011). This has me thinking of a systemic co-design strategy with a flexible set of starting points, regardless of the specific methods to be chosen. This approach will ideally bring a culture of receptiveness, inclusiveness and committedness (Cockton, 2009) by mixing perspectives and being empathic (Smeenk, 2019). Furthermore, in addition to structure, it will also bring energy and excitement, connect people and organisations, foster cross-pollination and lead to social, cultural, technological, ecological and economic change. In a nutshell, multi-value creation in value networks.

Below, I will discuss the four elements that play important roles in multi-value creation in these value networks, as well as in the development of a co-design tool such as the Co-Design Canvas. These are the concepts of: sphere of life; co-design; an empathic orientation; and a systemic orientation.

Sphere of life

As I mentioned earlier, the substantial number of grand societal challenges that now face us demand new approaches in collectively building alternative, sustainable futures. In addressing these challenges we must do so in a more integrated fashion and change our way of working together by forming so-called multi-stakeholder coalitions. In these coalitions each stakeholder, from his, her or its sphere of life, will then be able to play their respective roles and assume their responsibilities, with the results and credits being shared.

Stakeholders cannot resolve grand societal challenges as individual people or organisations, or by playing individualistic roles. Our nitrogen and energy crises, for example, cannot be tackled only on a personal or private level. Similarly, it is naïve to think that political action is all that is needed to take on the major polluters or make the transition to other types of energy. The goal is to help individual people, citizens, volunteers, politicians and entrepreneurs – in short, all spheres of life – see the bigger picture and thus act and change habits. And not only in moral terms, but in terms of the habits and conventions that make us, as stakeholders, unwilling or unable to make all kinds of choices.

Spheres of life Spheres of social interaction		Mechanisms/drivers Habits Patterns
Individual Personal	Personal	Selfless Love Friendship
	Private	Contract Achievement Reward
Collective Society	Political	Regulations Language Public interest
	Public	Freedom Spontaneous Shared

Table 1: Gudde's spheres of life (2016)

Many scholars think that there should be more collaboration in so-called quadruple helix or even quintuple helix (including non-human actors and nature) value networks for the purpose of addressing collective challenges. I prefer to think of these collaborations between citizens, commercial and non-profit organisations, knowledge institutions and governments as collaborations between four spheres of life: personal; public; private; and political (Gudde, 2016). These spheres of life (see Table 1) illustrate the influence that a stakeholder can exert in various roles – such as citizen, volunteer, politician and entrepreneur – in social life and in transforming society. For example, by day I work in a private setting to earn a living. In the late afternoon, I do volunteer work in a public setting to support the local soccer team. And in the evening, I return home to my personal environment to relax with my loved ones. Multi-spheres and multiple-values apply in these different contexts. In each context, a stakeholder can act differently in a responsible, social and environmentally friendly way (or otherwise). Furthermore, every sphere has its own habits, conventions and patterns of behaviour, drivers or mechanisms as it were. For example, in a personal sphere 'love' can be seen as a mechanism, while in a private sphere it might be more about 'contracts'. As stakeholders change spheres, their roles, perspectives and agency changes with them. Core values, on the other hand, remain in place across all four spheres. Even so, it is between these spheres of life where we will find societal challenges.

Each stakeholder thus has a role, responsibility and influence in the various spheres of life. Moreover, stakeholders can deploy the corresponding mechanisms for changing a problematic situation. It is exactly this that is key here, because it facilitates action (and the ability to re-imagine and rethink current habits) individually, and from more than one specific sphere. If all stakeholders are willing to commit

"The Canvas helps you to see and understand the bigger picture."

to acting from more than one sphere, it will be possible to instigate a shift. If stakeholders work together on the basis of the four spheres of life in a systemic, meaningful, ethical, empathic, inclusive and abductive manner, they will have a concrete set of guiding co-design elements. This will help facilitate parallel actions and get things moving towards a joint societal purpose. This multiple portfolio of actions or projects in the different spheres of life will provide a degree of overview and give stakeholders agency to change collectively.

The power of co-design

Design transforms current situations into preferred ones (Simon, 1996), whereas co-design can be defined as a democratic concept whereby people affected by design decisions are either involved in, or are part of, the shared design decision-making process (Sanoff, 1990). Moreover, co-design also makes use of collective creativity throughout the entire collaborative design process (Sanders & Stappers, 2008). It is a process in which stakeholders from various disciplines share their knowledge of both the design process and the design content (Kleinsmann & Valkenburg, 2008). In co-design, stakeholders work together towards a shared purpose and decide together what their journey will look like. Stakeholders' individual and collective interests, values, desires, experiences, and knowledge form the basis, so they must first be identified. After all, when focusing on areas that involve major societal challenges, there are no clear tasks or clients – or, should this actually be the case, we are all 'the client'.

The power of co-design lies in its focus on people and its ability to creatively influence and bridge gaps between different spheres of life, disciplines, domains and communities of practice. A co-design approach makes it possible to identify, share and come to grips with the different individual stakeholders' worldviews, values, experiences and latent and tacit knowledge, as well as their shared perspectives and ambitions. This enables stakeholders to create new bonds in potential value networks or so-called coalitions, and to co-imagine alternative futures and co-create multi-value. Furthermore, supported by abductive logic that is based on the values that people aspire to and their accompanying sphere of life drivers or mechanisms (see Table 1), co-designers can establish leverage points, develop surprising frames and reframes and take creative collective leaps that can lead to radical fundamental societal change.

Alongside imagination, visualisation and prototyping are what facilitate experimentation in and exploration of societal challenges. Tangibles and visuals can help as boundary objects or convivial tools between different communities of practice. And while they can be supportive as generative co-design means, they can also serve in preventing miscommunication. They take initially abstract thoughts and ideas and make them concrete, visible and tangible. They provide support in finding a common language, and facilitate the sharing, reflecting on, enriching and testing of first ideas and the like. These co-design means can be uniquely developed for the specific problematic situation at hand, or adapted from other fields. Think, for instance, of using collages, prototypes, design probes, videos, design games and scenarios. The discussions and joint elaborations between stakeholders about these practical and visual means ideally support them in making sense of the complexity and articulating personal values, knowledge, experiences and feelings.

They also help to leverage deep engagement, facilitate collaboration, unlock empathy, create shared understanding of values and mechanisms or drivers, and generate beneficial opportunities and frames for change in shared problematic situations. The subsequent design opportunities, leverage points and frames encourage and include new organisational co-design structures, accompanying approaches, coherent culture and social innovation. Next, I will discuss the important empathic aspects.

'unlock empathy'

An empathic orientation

Empathic design fuels our understanding of what is meaningful for people. And why that is meaningful for people. We use that understanding in co-design for shared decision making and designing (e.g., Fulton Suri, 2003; Koskinen & Battarbee, 2003; Kouprie & Sleeswijk Visser, 2009; Smeenk, 2019). It focuses on everyday life experiences and on individual values, desires, moods and emotions in human activities, human relations and interactions. Turning such affective experiences into understanding, inspiration and designs. Empathic design specifically addresses emotional, social and complex design challenges for, with, and between people. It suggests design approaches that consciously combine and balance objective and subjective mindsets, enabling designers and stakeholders to include relevant personal experiences and feelings.

Personal experiences and emotions influence stakeholders' interactions and relationships with each other and their intrinsic motivation for taking action, or not. A coalition of stakeholders will benefit from sharing their interests, values, aspirations, experiences and expertise in a timely manner, no matter how intimidating they might find that exchange at first. Empathy enables them to gain relevant and intimate insights, compassion and a deeper understanding of each other. We also know how important it is to share feelings of vulnerability, because doing so establishes a foundation for trust. If stakeholders dare to truly trust one another and be themselves within a collaboration, they can learn together

'dare to truly trust one another'

what is going on and what a given problematic situation calls for. This then leads to an awareness of relevant intentions, values and emotions. That awareness, or consciousness, then offers insights into how stakeholders respond as individuals and as a collective value network, as well as how they might respond differently in the future.

Empathy can be defined as people's intuitive ability to identify with others' life or lived experiences, such as thoughts, feelings, motivations, emotional and mental models, values, priorities, preferences and inner conflicts. Developing empathy is an individual process that grows during the course of a collaborative process. Empathy in this context is the ability to understand and feel compassion for the thoughts, experiences and emotions of other stakeholders and it enhances their ability to receive and process information. While psychologists hold different opinions as to an exact definition, they agree that empathy increases when people consciously alternate between directing their attention to themselves and to others, thereby consciously alternating between affective experiences and cognitive processes (Hess & Fila, 2016; Smeenk, 2019). In earlier research, I learned that empathy is a crucial precondition for societal impact design, because it elicits genuine emotional interest (EI), sensitivity (S) and self-awareness (SA) with regard to others (Smeenk, 2019). In such cases, empathy both informs us and inspires us to collaborate with other key stakeholders in realising positive societal change.

Empathic co-working means cultivating a mental habit of being aware of and reflecting on how you and other stakeholders are behaving and are being affected. This helps you understand what is going on below the surface. And this is irrespective of whether it is in connection with a problematic situation or the collaboration between partners

" It is important to create trust between policy makers and practitioners. It takes time, so start by openly sharing your goals, visions, and doubts without fear of showing vulnerability. "

Workshop participant

" We had a really good discussion. People got excited and stayed engaged – it was extremely inspiring! "

Participating citizen

" I think we initially communicated at different levels and had different expectations. If we would have had this Canvas at the beginning, at our first introduction, we would have gotten off to a much stronger start. "

Municipal official

" I think it is a brilliant way to have the big picture for a collaborative and inclusive, participatory process. "

Citizen science expert

" The Canvas playfully offers clarity and overview; it can help us talk to each other instead of about each other. "

Municipal policymaker

" The Canvas helped us to concretise our interests and to establish a common purpose and approach—we previously had no idea of what the other was doing and what we stood to gain from each other. "

Participating citizen

23

in a coalition or value network. Without empathic ability, it is impossible to understand what will drive stakeholders to force a change, or even prevent them from doing so. Similarly, without empathic ability it will not be possible to grasp why and how they are attached to ways, conventions and choices that are demonstrably contributing to the destruction of our world. Empathy gives us the ability to come to terms with the perspectives, values, needs and actions of other stakeholders, including the non-human variety, such as nature (without empathy, we would view nature as an opponent) and to understand and respect these stakeholders.

Empathic co-design is thus a complex and multifaceted phenomenon. Especially when conducted in multi-stakeholder settings, and aimed at multi-value creation and societal impact. Here, empathy is built among various stakeholders including the facilitators, designers and/or researchers. Given that societal challenges affect us all, individual people (such as citizens, entrepreneurs, volunteers and policymakers) and collectives (such as families, teams, organisations, neighbourhoods, networks, and society as a whole) will require shifts in different layers and spheres. It follows therefore that the empathic co-design process also needs a systemic orientation.

A systemic orientation

Systems thinking and systemic design has reclaimed some interest during the past ten years or so, as designers are confronted with new, large-scale challenges that involve multi-stakeholders. As a result of this, the term systemic co-design is also emerging. It is important to note here that one cannot say something is a system; you can only look at it as a system. In this respect, a system can be defined as a set of elements and relationships that operate in harmony towards the realisation of an overarching purpose or objective. Systems thinking is a comprehensive approach that goes beyond the individual and collective elements that are involved, to how these elements interrelate, how the system of which they are a part changes over time, and how it relates to a wider context. This approach is cross-cutting and system thinkers can identify multiple actors and factors that play a role in a challenge. They understand that systems are uncontrollable, so any intervention will set off another train of interaction which could positively reinforce a system. But what does it mean to look at dynamic problematic situations as a system? In what he calls a practical map, Stappers (2021) explains that three dimensions are key in systemic co-design processes. First of all, there is a common holistic understanding of the system structure: in other words how it hangs together. Secondly, there are the system dynamics: how it moves along. And thirdly, there is the (facilitated) interaction within the change process: how you may, or may not, be able to direct it.

In systemic co-design for societal change, we therefore look for places in complex systems where a small shift could lead to fundamental change in the system as a whole. Spheres of life mechanisms and drivers are crucial in effecting these small shifts that, together, culminate in change. These so-called leverage points (Meadows, 1999) can be seen as the mechanisms in the creative abduction act for change (Dorst, 2010). I will explain abduction in more detail at page 26. Intervention and experimentation in the problematic situation is at its most effective when done at these leverage points, where key relationships meet. Up till now, it is the people (individuals and collectives) that have needed to make these shifts. Therefore, it is important to understand aspects such as their perspectives, implicit worldviews, experiences, values, interests and behaviours, as they might be the leverage points that will instigate the shift that will make profound change possible. This is the kind of view that the Co-Design Canvas will ideally facilitate. It is a tool that will enable a coalition to be honest about their problematic system and the elements and relationships involved. In this respect it is an instrument that will facilitate how a coalition can frame or reframe a problematic situation. Systems thinking can give multi-stakeholders a common language that reconciles inputs from various disciplines and spheres of life, facilitates their collaboration, and helps them to describe and visualise things, and perhaps even understand, predict and improve how those things are seen and how they are intertwined. This way of looking at things gives stakeholders a possible shared purpose and overview of the system to work on and work with.

Towards the CO-DESIGN CANVAS

While complex challenges explicitly point to the existence of a diversity in aspirations and interests of the different domains, communities of practices and spheres of life, agendas and visions are ambiguous. This makes the nature of empathic and systemic co-design processes multi-layered and less easy to oversee. As such, their outcomes and outputs are unforeseeable. This uncertainty is difficult to embrace, particularly for non-designers such as stakeholders from other domains and design novices such as design students. Sometimes, these people get nervous about change. They want to speed things up, see the opportunities ASAP and make sure that they are there in time. Given the complexity of a typical co-design challenge, multi-stakeholder coalitions often face difficulties when carrying it out. Initiating stakeholders or facilitators, as well as others,

are often at a loss to know where and how to start their journey together, not to mention which role they should take or which facilitation and (reciprocal) encounters to organise. Moreover, they implicitly or explicitly struggle with whom they should involve and how to avoid other, marginalised stakeholders feeling that they are being overlooked. Furthermore, they wonder how best to create a learning environment that will foster people's collective wisdom and creativity, make stakeholders take ownership and realise profound social innovation together.

Problems in collaborative processes often arise from tensions between the people, teams, departments and organisations that are involved. Because of the pressure of time, for example, or conflicting interests and power imbalances, or evolving (social) contingencies that were neither foreseen nor discussed beforehand. Without a shared working method, culture, structure and a common vocabulary, coalitions may find it difficult to work on change together, which is why we have developed and are introducing the Co-Design Canvas and its Manual. Using the Canvas can clarify these issues and relationships and offer stakeholders a common language and methodology to use in and on the process. The Co-Design Canvas can help facilitate all these processes and throw light on why processes sometimes succeed and other times fail. You can read more about this in the following chapters.

Abduction

Abduction differs from induction and deduction. While all three pertain to the logic of scientific thinking, deductive research is the logic used in comparative research. A research team will typically search through literature to form a picture of a given challenge, on the basis of which they will then formulate and test hypotheses. Inductive research, meanwhile, is bottom-up research. By observing, exploring and asking questions, the research team will formulate a theory. With abduction, the research team will alternate between theorising about what is going on and testing whether their assumptions are correct. This thinking resembles design. Dorst (2011) defined the concept of abduction in design, as it relates to open-ended wicked challenges, as follows: The sum of 'what' and 'how' is 'value'. Abduction is then an iterative and creative process of exploring, creating, testing and adjusting 'how' and 'value' combination possibilities, which Dorst called frames. The idea is that, provided enough frames (combining different values with different mechanisms) are considered, identified and weighed-up against one another, the most desirable and realistic alternative futures will inevitably emerge in the 'what'. For his part, Cockton (2009) said: 'The context of choice makes it credible'. Yet, this begs the question: 'How can we find these multiple frames (with which to experiment) consisting of latent individual and collective values and accompanying sphere-of-life mechanisms?'

Design needs to adopt new, flexible strategies that support stakeholders like non-designers in adaptively and empathically responding to dynamic and systemic contexts and value-network collaborations.

3

How the Canvas came into being

The Co-Design Canvas unfolded in the context of an European Horizon 2020 research project[2]. The aim of this research project was to experiment with new co-design methodologies, co-discover opportunities for local challenges, and stimulate bottom-up initiatives in ten pilots across Europe. In the Netherlands, the project was led by the design museum in Kerkrade, to address questions relating to the quality of life in a small, ageing and shrinking Dutch village. The objective was to discover how participatory policymaking can stimulate bottom-up initiatives, and vice versa, by developing tools. These tools had to increase citizen engagement, make the community more future-proof and inject more confidence into multi-stakeholder collaborations. Citizens, policymakers, and the museum formed a multi-stakeholder coalition for this project and I lent my support as a designer and researcher.

What soon became clear in the project was that the existing collaboration between citizens and policymakers was not effective and it was leading to tensions. Both sides indicated that they missed knowledge, guidance and a means of jointly addressing societal challenges. They needed a tool that would support their collaboration on a more equal and transparent footing, in partnership and based on trust. Only then would it be possible for citizen initiatives to grow and flourish and to realise the desired change. The coalition between the two sides needed more focus and shared priorities,

as well as a good alignment of their contrasting interests and responsibilities, taking into account the municipality's organisational possibilities and limitations, structure and decision-making processes. The situation called for a validated and practical co-design process instrument to guide them towards an energetic and new way of working together, effectively. Based on this practice, and inspired by the academic article 'Design Choices Framework for Co-Creation' by Lee et al. (2018) (see Figure 1), the seeds for the Co-Design Canvas were sown.

> The Co-Design Canvas can be used by multiple stakeholders when planning, conducting, and evaluating a co-design process in a variety of contexts. The Canvas comprises eight co-design decision cards. Together, these provide an overview of, and inject structure into, a set of relevant co-design decisions in which individual and collective stakeholders can be recognised, heard, and empowered on an equal footing.

2   This work was supported by the European Union's Horizon 2020 Research and Innovation programme, under grant agreement No. 788217. www.siscodeproject.eu

A. Involving stakeholders with diverse kmowledge leads to a more open-ended brief and reframes the purpose of change of the project.

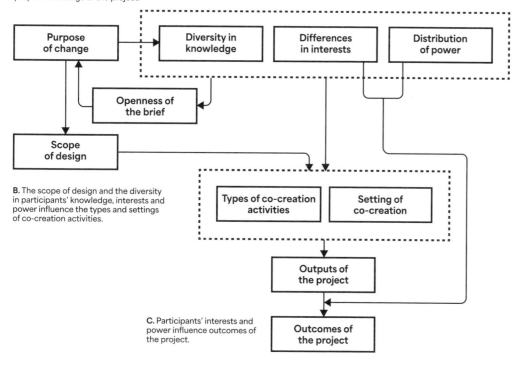

B. The scope of design and the diversity in participants' knowledge, interests and power influence the types and settings of co-creation activities.

C. Participants' interests and power influence outcomes of the project.

Figure 1: The relationships in the Design Choices Framework for Co-Creation Projects (Lee et al., 2018, page 28)

The Design Choices Framework

The process flow model of Lee et al. (2018) comprises ten co-design decisions, namely: the purpose of the change; the openness of the brief; the scope; diversity in knowledge; differences in interest; the distribution of power; the type of co-creation activities; the co-creation setting; the output; and the outcome (see Figure 1). This model gives design research an insightful structure and vocabulary that can help to explain what kind of key dimensions co-design challenges are built upon, what influences the formulation of these processes, and what it is that fuels the selection and development of working approaches and co-design activities. Moreover, it can provide an overview and help to plan and assess a co-design process by giving a more systemic understanding of the key attributes, dimensions and co-design decisions in processes that are governed by social contingencies. Finally, the framework reveals influential relationships between the different decisions, pointing to an iterative and complex process in which many dynamic design elements need to be taken into account.

Co-design decisions can be seen as a concept to be shared. They cut across vocabularies, domains and spheres of life and as such can bridge the gap between research and practice. Moreover, decisions are less abstract than design principles and more generic than activities or methods. As such, they can be a way for stakeholders to find common ground and provide an outline for co-design processes.

Although we were greatly inspired by Lee's framework, as it distinguishes clear and practical co-design decisions for stakeholder coalitions, its visual representation was seen as somewhat abstract. Understanding this framework might be hard for those who were new to co-design, such as design students or non-designer stakeholders from other domains. It was deemed that the visual reproduction as a flowchart might not be the appropriate way to disseminate and communicate this knowledge in practice. The coalition seemed to need a less-complicated, practical and attractive representation in a more-appropriate medium. Moreover, some of Lee's vocabulary and terminology (such as project, participants, customers, target group) did not do justice to the transformative, more pro-active context in which multi-stakeholder coalitions take ownership of a process and intrinsically work together to realise societal impact. Clearly, the concept needed to be tested, tweaked and complemented to convert it into a more appealing, playful, and practical intermediate-level knowledge tool. And one that could be used for both practical and educational purposes, with a specific focus on tackling societal challenges in multi-stakeholder collaborations.

Since its inception, the Co-Design Canvas and its Manual have been shared extensively, via the website of the University of Applied Sciences and the EU H2020 consortium for example, See the two QR-codes on this page. The Canvas has also been presented at various conferences, and has been used in several practices, education and research environments. The application period of the Canvas can range from a 90-minute workshop to a project lasting several months. The settings in which it can be used vary from online webinars, streamed and live conferences, online in Miro or Mural collaboration tools and offline in co-design sessions, workshops and training courses. In an educational setting, the Canvas enables students and teachers to plan, analyse and evaluate their co-design projects with partners from the real world in living labs. Moreover, in educational training programmes and workshops, the Canvas is widely used for helping creative student teams and tutors to understand empathic co-design and for building empathic co-design capacity. In practice and research, it enables new coalitions of collaborative partners to get off to a good start by managing expectations and consolidating prior knowledge. Furthermore, we have since learned that the Canvas and its Manual are also relevant beyond design practices and can be used in sectors that include tourism, healthcare and chemistry among others. In the following paragraphs, we will discuss each of the four categories in the Co-Design Canvas and their accompanying eight cards.

Inholland web

SISCODE web

In our EU H2020 research project, the assumption was that the citizens would recognise the proposed aspects of the framework of Lee et al. (2018) in their local collaborative processes. The new, to-be-developed instrument would connect all the design decisions that define and affect a co-design process. During the project, several things in Lee's original framework were changed. First of all, the vocabulary or terminology had to be made as easy to understood as possible for both the citizens and policymakers, as well as across their different communities of practices. To this end, we decided to rename the original framework the 'Co-Design Canvas'. Secondly, citizens came up with additional card terms, which were not included in Lee's original process flow, such as the 'Who are we missing?' stakeholder-card element. Thirdly, we injected a systemic element into the Canvas. We noticed that citizens discussed their own contrasting interests, knowledge and power dynamics as opposed to those of the policymakers, and vice versa. There were even differences between an individual alderman and a strategic policymaker within the same municipality. For this reason, in the stakeholder card of the Co-Design Canvas a trigger was introduced to include the personal interests, knowledge and power of each stakeholder (individual perspective) as well as that of the team, organisation or coalition (group perspective). This actually added fresh knowledge to Lee's original framework.

The idea of the Canvas - in this form - came from the citizens. They were inspired by the well-known visual form of the Business Model Canvas (BMC) of Osterwalder & Pigneur (2010)[3]. By using this structure, in their eyes the Canvas became appealing and usable in practice. Moreover, a conscious choice was made to develop loose cards that collectively form the Co-Design Canvas. After noticing that the citizens and policymakers moved back and forth through these cards, when designing the Canvas we took care to encourage this element of iterative refinement in its content. For example, if stakeholders know more about one another's knowledge, interests and power, as well as that of others, they seem to be more able to establish a joint purpose and aspire for concrete results. For usability and practical purposes, all separate cards were made printable on regular A3 and A4 printers. The citizens also made it clear that they would appreciate a user manual.

---

3   The BMC is a well-known visual tool for exploring and designing new business models. It includes separate building blocks that together give an overview of the ingredients of business modelling and the process that is involved (Osterwalder & Pigneur, 2010)

The coalition enjoyed working with this newly developed instrument and greatly appreciated the overview it provided. They described the final Co-Design Canvas as: 'A concrete, clear, visually attractive, but also playful tool that can be used for different types of challenges'. According to them, the value of the Canvas lies primarily in its shared vocabulary, shared decision-making, process overview, and the consistently open and transparent dialogue about one another's aspirations, interests, knowledge and position. Putting certain aspects on the agenda led to an in-depth and honest discussion. For example, regarding the extent of each stakeholder's influence, it was seen as taboo-breaking to talk about power. The citizens acknowledged that there was more trust between them and more vulnerability towards each other, and that a fresh citizen perspective also brings with it a certain power. Moreover, they experienced their sessions with others and with their fellow citizens as 'fun, inspiring, and energetic', and that their conversations just kept on going. The Canvas, they added, gave them fresh insights and provided a shared language and mutual understanding of the challenge at hand. In one case, it was conceded that the Canvas brought new stakeholders to the table, stakeholders who were previously unaware of each other's roles in the challenge they collectively faced. Furthermore, all citizens lauded the fact that the Canvas helped them to keep track of the co-design process: 'We now know what to expect'. The policymakers, meanwhile, insisted that addressing fundamental aspects in any collaboration, such as the co-design decisions, helps define a clear starting point and a common vision. It goes without saying that the interests and ambitions of every stakeholder are not the same, but by sharing and openly discussing their different perspectives at the beginning makes it easier to find common ground. The Canvas then helps participants see and understand the bigger picture. What's more, they felt, the Canvas can not only be applied to the citizens' own local community, for which it was designed, but in a more generic context too. They were convinced that their participation in this research project had delivered meaningful results.

For more in detailed information about how the Co-Design Canvas was developed, in theory and in practice, I suggest you read these two academic articles:

- Smeenk, W. (2023). Empathic CO-DESIGN CANVAS: A tool for supporting multistakeholder co-design processes. International Journal of Design.
- Smeenk, W., Zielhuis, M. & Van Turnhout, K. (2023). Understanding the research-practice gap in design research: a comparison of four perspectives.

The CO-DESIGN CANVAS categories

In addition to the framework of Lee et al. (2018), practical experiences were the inspiration for co-developing the Co-Design Canvas in the context of the EU H2020 real-life setting. In this project, we investigated whether the co-design variables of Lee's framework were recognised in practice and how we could use them in a tool that would support the coalition.

In conjunction with the stakeholders, the ensuing Co-Design Canvas was developed, validated, reworked and transformed into an actionable form. This resulted in two intermediate-level knowledge products: the Co-Design Canvas and the Manual (Smeenk, Köppchen & Bertrand, 2021). The Canvas thus represents validated and proven co-design theory that can be used in design practice and for design education in an eminently appropriate way.

The Co-Design Canvas comprises four categories inspired by, and based on, Lee et al. (2018). These four categories are:

· the Preconditions (WHY)
· the Stakeholders (WHO)
· the Ends (WHAT)
· and the Means (HOW)

Moreover, eight co-design decision cards collectively comprise the Co-Design Canvas as a whole. It is important to note here that the relationships between the cards are more important than the individual cards and that iteration through the Canvas and its cards is key. See also the new process flow of the cards in Figure 2.

The Canvas comes with a Manual, which is to be found in Chapter 4. The Manual describes the Co-Design Canvas and its cards and includes background information, as well as guiding tips on its facilitation and accompanying tools. I will discuss the Co-Design Canvas cards per category in the following pages.

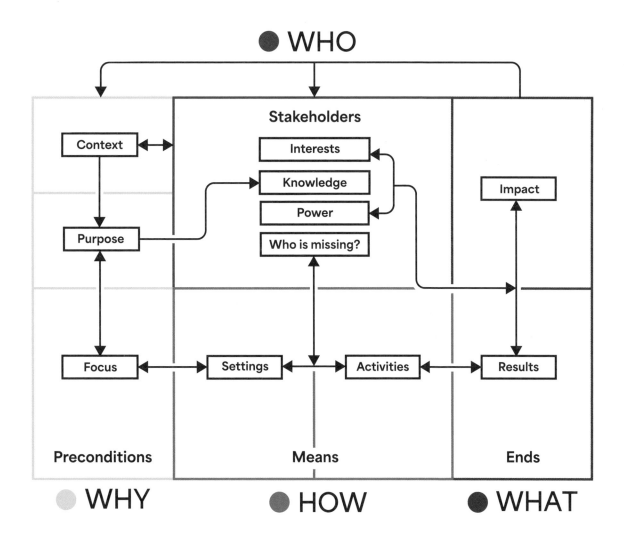

Figure 2: The Co-Design Canvas comprises four categories and eight cards

WHY Co-Design Preconditions

The Preconditions category of the Co-Design Canvas sets the scene for starting up the co-design process and framing the overall context, purpose and focus of the project: **Why are we starting a co-design initiative?** These preconditions comprise the following three yellow cards positioned on the left side of the Canvas: the co-design Context, Purpose and Focus cards. For more information about this, see pages 62-67 of the Manual in Chapter 4. Moreover, the co-design Context feeds the co-design Purpose and the co-design Focus (see Figure 2). Each is discussed in more detail below.

Co-Design Context

Co-design processes in a societal challenge revolve around a problematic context. They have an open-ended character and involve many different stakeholders. The co-design Context card is positioned at the top-left corner of the Canvas because the problematic context of a societal challenge forms the natural 'starting point' of a co-design process. Subsequently, the problematic situation, or context, asks for a desired joint purpose.

Co-Design Purpose

To open up discussions on what can be done about the problematic context, the stakeholders will search for a joint purpose. These discussions can be about experiences on a people level, in culture on an organisational level and/or in a collaboration network on a system cross-organisational level. To this end, the Purpose card emphasises the necessity of the transformation. The co-design purpose - supported by inspiring and ambitious narratives - can motivate the

stakeholders in their roles in the co-design process. A purpose is all about agenda setting, vision, and long-term decisions. It links closely with the Impact card, which is discussed later. The Purpose card is positioned at the centre-left of the Canvas.

Co-Design Focus

The Focus card defines the direction to be taken by the co-design process, but it does not stipulate requirements. At this stage, this card is still very explorative and aims to establish what questions need to be asked and addressed during the co-design activities. The Focus card encourages stakeholders to define several sub-design questions formulated, for example, as: 'How can we... in order to...?' or 'How might we... to ensure that ...?' These sub-questions, along with an accompanying portfolio of sub-projects executed by sub-teams, can lead to multi-value creation and to the wished-for impact. Defining these sub-questions and forming sub-teams enables the coalition to work towards their joint purpose, leading to several concrete results and, eventually, the desired impact. The sub-questions in the Focus card serve as a starting point for various design activities that can be used in parallel and in associated settings. Herewith, the Focus card is all about framing and reframing and can be seen as the synthesis card of the top end of the Canvas. Physically, this card is positioned at the bottom-left corner of the Canvas.

.

● WHO Co-Design Stakeholders

The Stakeholders category in the Co-Design Canvas is relevant in societal challenges because every stakeholder has different interests and represents a part of the puzzle that will eventually lead to change. This category invites stakeholders to discuss: **Who has which knowledge, interest and power?** Everyone must take ownership of the transformation that they jointly want to realise. Aligning expectations from the start is important. The red Stakeholders card is positioned at the top-centre of the Canvas and serves as its beating heart. The Stakeholders card differentiates four design decisions, decisions: interests, knowledge, power and who is missing. All these elements can be discussed from both individual and collective perspectives. Furthermore, the stakeholders' various interests, diversity of knowledge, distribution of power, and who is missing, feeds the co-design Context card and the co-design Means, the co-design Ends categories (see Figure 2).

Stakeholder Interests
In tackling societal challenges through co-design, stakeholders can have shared, different or conflicting interests. Or perhaps no interests at all. Addressing these differences makes stakeholders conscious of their variety, the undercurrent and the consequent complexity. By engaging with one another and exchanging differences in motivations and interests, mutual understanding between stakeholders will increase.

Stakeholder Knowledge
In all likelihood, stakeholders will have a diversity in knowledge. To achieve concrete results and impact in the long-run, stakeholders need to be aware of who can provide what relevant experiential knowledge and mandatory expertise knowledge. The former offers real-life experience, while the latter can include, among other things, process, organisational or thematic expertise.

Stakeholder Power
Being acutely aware of your own power and role and explicitly addressing omnipresent stakeholders' power dynamics and unequal power relationships openly, at an early stage of the co-design process, can make coalitions more effective. It might prevent power imbalances from leading to misunderstandings and insensitive decisions. It can also provide new insights into the various (f)actors that are involved in power, such as strength, influence, capacity, ownership, willingness, network and support. Power in this context means more than financial clout, decision-making or legal status. Sometimes people can feel powerless. Exercising your power or, conversely, not exercising it, can affect the co-design activities and its settings. And this, by extension, can influence the concrete results and impact. If stakeholders do not take the responsibility that comes with their respective roles, they might frustrate or hinder any progress.

Who is missing
It is important to ascertain whether anyone is missing at the table. Someone, who could help with their knowledge, expertise, experience, power or influence, and thus make it easier to realise the desired change? Which individuals, groups or organisations have an interest, knowledge or power, yet are not represented? This card is positioned at the foot of the Stakeholders card.

● WHAT Co-Design Ends

The Co-Design Ends category of the Canvas reveals what the co-design process leads to in terms of the intangible, more long-term impact, as well as the more-tangible, concrete, short-term results. This category invites stakeholders to discuss: **What should we collaboratively create?** The Ends category involves two explicit design decisions: concrete immediate results and the desired impact. These cards are blue and positioned one above the other on the right side of the Canvas (see Figure 2). Both the Impact and the Results cards are discussed in more detail below.

Co-Design Results

The concrete Results card pertains to short-term decisions and involves the immediate results and deliverables to further implement. These results range from idea directions to artefacts, from scenarios to services, and new participatory policymaking working processes that are established by the stakeholders, either together or in separate teams. The Results card is positioned at the bottom-right corner of the Canvas because it is related to the Focus card, which is also positioned at the bottom on the left of the Canvas.

Co-Design Impact

The Impact card pertains to outcomes, or so-called impacts of the co-design process as a whole. Transformation and impact require time, stamina, staying power, and vision. They go beyond concrete results. Impact ranges from new mindsets to culture, from symbiotic relationships to economic aspects, from societal to environmental impact and to behavioural and system change. The Impact card is positioned at the top-right corner of the Canvas because it is related to the Context card, which is also positioned at the top on the left of the Canvas.

● HOW Co-Design Means

The Co-Design Means category of the Canvas reveals and explicates the activities and settings of the process of **how to co-design.** To this end, the Means category involves two explicit design decisions: Activities and Settings. Both of these decisions depend on the project preconditions and stakeholders and what the settings should be to achieve the desired ends. These cards are green and positioned alongside one another at the bottom-centre of the Canvas see, Figure 2. Both the Activities and Settings cards are discussed in more detail below.

Co-Design Activities

The Activities card pertains to the types of activity to choose or develop with regard to the co-design project preconditions and its stakeholders. The activities are meant to relate to and are specifically set up to answer each sub-question raised in the Focus card. Each activity involves a specific learning setting and a sub-group of stakeholders matching each question and accompanying quest. The Activities card is positioned between the Settings card and the Results card at the bottom-centre of the Canvas because it relates to both. The type of activities are aimed at eliciting stakeholders' interests, knowledge and power, and generating design opportunities by generative co-design means.

Co-Design Settings

The Settings card pertains to the type of learning environment that is required to achieve the desired co-design ends. The activities require an accompanying, online, physical or material setting for co-learning. The Settings card is positioned between the Focus and Activities cards at the bottom-centre of the Canvas because it relates to both. The choice of a setting influences the activities.

The Canvas can be seen as an intermediate-level knowledge product on three levels:

1. As a research instrument: the Co-Design Canvas elicits knowledge about the perspectives, and personal and professional lives of its stakeholders
2. As a participation instrument: the Co-Design Canvas allows stakeholders to influence their own lives, thereby emancipating and democratising them
3. As an educative instrument: the Co-Design Canvas builds empathic co-design capacity among stakeholders

4

The CO-DESIGN CANVAS Manual

The Co-Design Canvas is a tool for initiating, planning, conducting and assessing collaborations around societal challenges with various stakeholders openly and transparently. It offers a means for all spheres of life, the (semi-)public and the private sector to communicate and collaborate clearly. Think of government officials, citizens, business professionals, NGOs, educators, researchers and the Canvas can even include non-humans as nature if appropriate.

From the start, the Canvas clarifies differences in interests, diversity in knowledge and experiences, and distribution of power. The Canvas focuses on the desired positive impact and concrete results, and ensures that everyone's voice is truly heard. In short, the Canvas is a tool that makes the variables of a co-design process clear and open to discussion, creating a common language, a clear starting point and an understanding of each other's role and responsibility. The Canvas provides the flexibility to respond to unexpected events and the knowledge to better understand, conduct, plan and assess a co-design project.

'The Canvas is a means. Completing the Canvas is not a goal in itself'

One page, eight cards

The Co-Design Canvas specifically identifies eight variables that influence a co-design process: the co-design Context, Purpose, Stakeholders, Results, Impact, Focus, Setting, and Activities. These variables do not only affect the process as a whole, but are also interrelated. The co-design stakeholders influence the co-design focus, which, in turn, determines who should participate in the process. The stakeholders then also determine which concrete results and impact are desired and feasible.

The Co-Design Canvas integrates these variables into co-design process element cards, together forming one page making it an accessible tool for co-design projects. Each variable corresponds to one card. The top of the canvas is primarily about taking stock and exploring the problematic current context (why) and who should (ideally) be involved. The bottom side of the Canvas focuses on which co-design activities will be conducted with whom and where (how) to create opportunities for concrete results and positive impact (what).

How to use the CO-DESIGN CANVAS?

When using the Co-Design Canvas, it is important to realise that the Canvas is primarily a means to determine the focus of the following co-design process (setting and activities) to achieve the desired concrete results and impact. Completing the Canvas is not a goal in itself.

In the Co-Design Canvas, the problematic context and the initial purpose of change, which together comprise the current situation (why), almost always form the starting point for collaboration. Throughout the process, you constantly move back and forth between the desired impact and concrete results (what), the stakeholders involved (who), the co-design focus, and its setting and activities (how).

Working on the top cards of the Canvas results in a sharper co-design focus, while you may also discover that the actual problematic context is much broader or more complex, and that you need to adjust the desired impact and concrete results accordingly. The Canvas is a dynamic tool whose content is constantly changing. Finally, a co-design project is an iterative and joint learning process.

The Canvas works best when printed or projected on a large surface: think of an A1 poster on the wall or a big carpet on the floor. In this way, the Canvas as a whole really comes to live and stakeholders can sketch, discuss and walk over the important co-design cards using Post-it memo's, tangible objects, etc.

The eight cards have different sizes: the co-design Context is an A5 Size Landscape, the Purpose an A5 Landscape Size, the Focus an A4 Portrait Size, the Stakeholders an A3 Landscape Size, the Activities an A4 Portrait Size, the Settings an A4 Size Portrait, the Results an A4 Size Portrait and the Impact card an A4 Portrait Size. The cards can be printed on any standard A3/A4-printer and are provided under a Creative Commons license and to be found on the website via the QR code on this page.

Inholland web

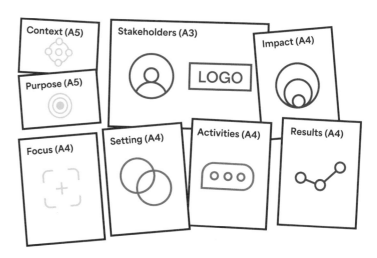

Figure 3: Card sizes

46

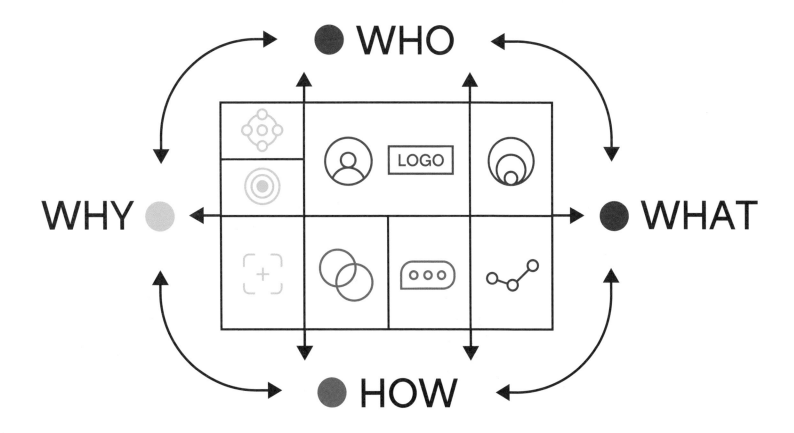

Figure 4: The Co-Design Canvas comprises four categories and eight cards

The CO-DESIGN CANVAS

On the next pages you will find the
Co-Design Canvas front and back side

The CO-DESIGN CANVAS front

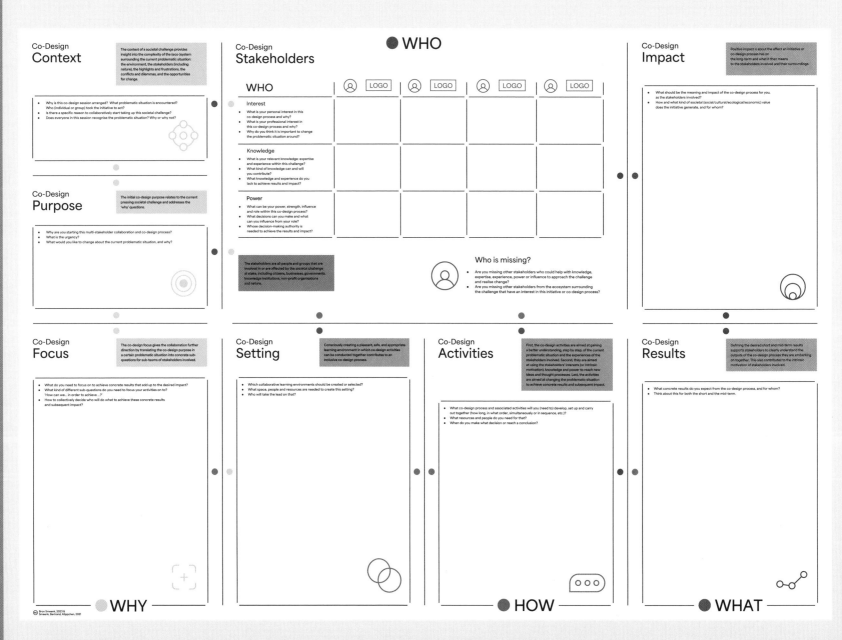

Co-Design Context

The context of a societal challenge provides insight into the complexity of the (eco-)system surrounding the current problematic situation: the environment, the stakeholders (including nature), the highlights and frustrations, the conflicts and dilemmas, and the opportunities for change.

- Why is this co-design session arranged? What problematic situation is encountered?
- Who (individual or group) took the initiative to act?
- Is there a specific reason to collaboratively start taking up this societal challenge?
- Does everyone in this session recognise the problematic situation? Why or why not?

Co-Design Purpose

The initial co-design purpose relates to the current pressing societal challenge and addresses the 'why' questions.

- Why are you starting this multi-stakeholder collaboration and co-design process?
- What is the urgency?
- What would you like to change about the current problematic situation, and why?

● WHO

Co-Design Stakeholders

WHO

	👤 LOGO	👤 LOGO	👤 LOGO	👤 LOGO

Interest
- What is your personal interest in this co-design process and why?
- What is your professional interest in this co-design process and why?
- Why do you think it is important to change the problematic situation around?

Knowledge
- What is your relevant knowledge, expertise and experience within this challenge?
- What kind of knowledge can and will you contribute?
- What knowledge and experience do you lack to achieve results and impact?

Power
- What can be your power, strength, influence and role within this co-design process?
- What decisions can you make and what can you influence from your role?
- Whose decision-making authority is needed to achieve the results and impact?

The stakeholders are all people and groups that are involved in or are affected by the societal challenge at stake, including citizens, businesses, governments, knowledge institutions, non-profit organisations and nature.

Who is missing?

- Are you missing other stakeholders who could help with knowledge, expertise, experience, power or influence to approach the challenge and realise change?
- Are you missing other stakeholders from the ecosystem surrounding the challenge that have an interest in this initiative or co-design process?

Co-Design Impact

Positive impact is about the effect an initiative or co-design process has on the long-term and what it then means to the stakeholders involved and their surroundings.

- What should be the meaning and impact of the co-design process for you, as the stakeholders involved?
- How and what kind of societal (social/cultural/ecological/economic) value does the initiative generate, and for whom?

Co-Design Focus

The co-design focus gives the collaboration further direction by translating the co-design purpose in a certain problematic situation into concrete sub-questions for sub-teams of stakeholders involved.

- What do you need to focus on to achieve concrete results that add up to the desired impact?
- What kind of different sub-questions do you need to focus your activities on to? 'How can we... in order to achieve ...?'
- How to collectively decide who will do what to achieve these concrete results and subsequent impact?

Co-Design Setting

Consciously creating a pleasant, safe, and appropriate learning environment in which co-design activities can be conducted together contributes to an inclusive co-design process.

- Which collaborative learning environments should be created or selected?
- What space, people and resources are needed to create this setting?
- Who will take the lead on that?

Co-Design Activities

First, the co-design activities are aimed at gaining a better understanding, step by step, of the current problematic situation and the experiences of the stakeholders involved. Second, they are aimed at using the stakeholders' interests (or intrinsic motivation), knowledge and power to reach new ideas and thought processes. Last, the activities are aimed at changing the problematic situation to achieve concrete results and subsequent impact.

- What co-design process and associated activities will you (need to) develop, set up and carry out together (how long, in what order, simultaneously or in sequence, etc.)?
- What resources and people do you need for that?
- When do you make what decision or reach a conclusion?

Co-Design Results

Defining the desired short and mid-term results supports stakeholders to clearly understand the outputs of the co-design process they are embarking on together. This also contributes to the intrinsic motivation of stakeholders involved.

- What concrete results do you expect from the co-design process, and for whom?
- Think about this for both the short and the mid-term.

WHY ——— ● HOW ——— ● WHAT ———

Bron Smeenk, 2023 & Smeenk, Bertrand, Köppchen, 2021

The CO-DESIGN CANVAS back

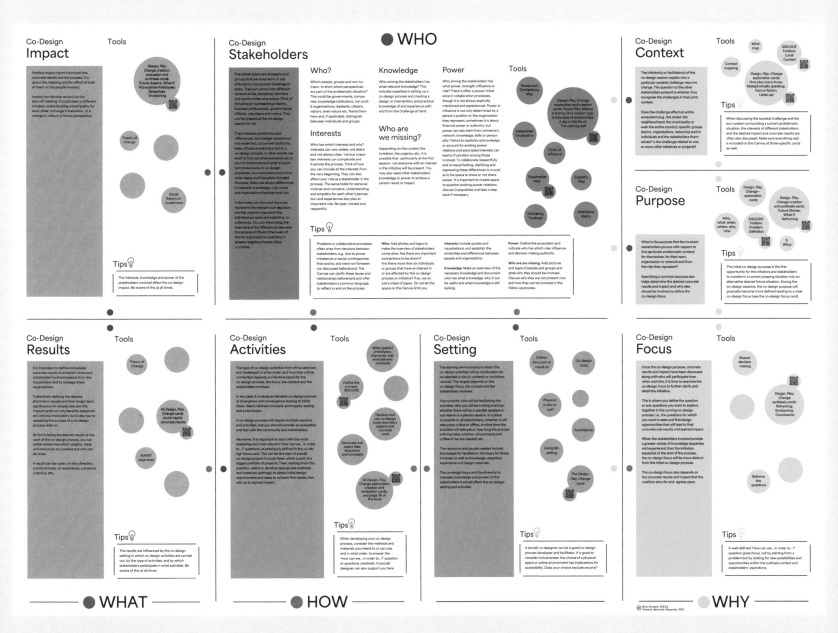

Additional Co-Design Tools

The back of each Co-Design Canvas card explains that specific card's purpose and background. There are also suggestions for additional tools and tips to get you started.

There is a wide variety of design tools, most of which are also available online. These are all tools to help you think in a certain way and/or to facilitate your co-design process. The efficacy of these tools always depends on the specific situation and the preference and knowledge of the stakeholders or facilitators.

Some of the Co-Design Canvas cards refer to co-design methods mentioned in my book and game 'Design, Play, Change', a playful introduction to design thinking with serious chances for change. Moreover, some of the proposed tools are included in the SISCODE toolbox, see QR code below. Additionally, the cards tap into other proven methods and toolkits which are available online, such as the Design Method Toolkit by the Digital Society School, see QR code below.

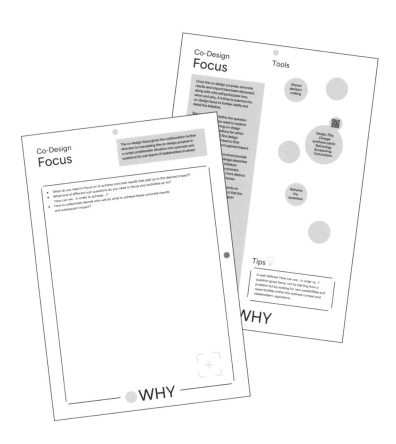

Figure 5: Co-Design Canvas card: front and back side

Toolkit DSS

SISCODE toolbox

Design, Play, Change

holders are all peop and
izations that participate in or are
by the initiative, including citizens
governments, knowledge
and non-profit organisations. They
know the following of each
Logo
Logo
Logo

Practical guidance

In co-design and participation processes, you want to empower every person to have equal input; you want everyone's voice to be heard and included. However, there are always differences in interests, experience, knowledge, role, social and organisational background, etc. The Canvas aims to obtain insight into these differences and similarities through open, respectful and transparent dialogues and by developing a collaborative approach. How you facilitate this conversation is at least as important as who joins the co-design process.

Online and offline

This Co-Design Canvas Manual is based on an interactive and creative co-design session in a physical setting. While an online setting is certainly possible, it introduces new challenges and requires additional competencies and conditions e.g., web conferencing software, such as Zoom or Microsoft Teams, and interactive collaboration programmes, such as Miro or Mural.

Time

A good dialogue takes time. You will need at least 90 minutes to three hours to discuss most of the Canvas cards. Take your time, but stay within limits. Decide in advance how much time to allow for each card and complete it in time: avoid unnecessary repetition and getting bogged down in discussions resulting in loss of motivation. Tip: set an alarm for 20 minutes per card, for example.

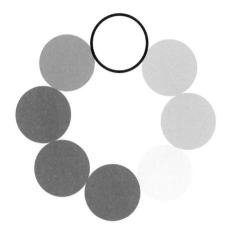

Facilitation

It can be a good idea to have one person facilitate the session, while the others discuss and 'fill' in the Canvas cards and thoroughly document the discussion that way. Post-its can be useful here. But avoid only words, you can also make drawings or use clay or plasticide, for example. This working method allows everyone to write or draw out their thoughts individually before exchanging ideas, providing a multitude of perspectives and ensuring that everyone gets a chance to express their views. Afterwards a clustering can be appropriate and insightful. In most cases, one of the stakeholders can act as a facilitator. However, in some case it may be helpful to enlist an independent facilitator, depending on the level of knowledge and experience required for the session, and the difference a facilitator can make. For example, the facilitator plays a role in creating and maintaining a pleasant, open and safe atmosphere (the co-design setting). A social designer can also help the coalition to gather new insights through design methods such as the ones explained in my earlier book Design, Play, Change (2022).

Iterative process

Use the Co-Design Canvas flexibly. The Canvas comprises eight interrelated co-design cards. The order of the cards is not fixed. They can be used individually or in combination with each other. The connection icons in the margin (see Figure 7) show how the cards can be combined. See also the overview in Figure 6. You can and will use the Canvas multiple times during different phases of the co-design process - initially to explore the challenge with a small group, later to determine the co-design focus with a more complete team of stakeholders. You can then split up again and explore the sub-questions in sub-groups and sub-sessions.

Step by step

Preparation

Initiative and organization

A good co-design session requires preparation, both in terms of the content of the societal challenge or initiative, and in terms of the physical parameters in which the discussion takes place. Make an inventory of potential stakeholders and identify the ideal partners with whom to realise change. The invitation is also important. How you invite the potential stakeholders determines who will come; the tone of voice, the location, the time -even how and where you disseminate the invitation- all have an impact. It is important to get the stakeholders excited about the content and make it clear that their voices matter for positive change.

Start

Welcome and introduction

In preparation for the first co-design session, the initiator(s) or facilitator(s) can already complete parts of the Canvas from their perspective. This can be used as the starting point of a dialogue, but it does not have to be: you can also start with a blank Co-Design Canvas. You always start a Canvas session by welcoming the participants. Thank them for taking the time to be there. It is good to hold a round of introductions if the stakeholders involved do not know each other. An introduction round may also provide information relevant to the Canvas. You can even use the Canvas Impact card for this introduction. Introduce yourself with a metaphorical drawing of what you dream of? The outcomes can already be positioned in the relevant fields on the Canvas. However, keep the introduction round short, as the time is also needed for the dialogue about the other content, during which people will also get to know each other better. You can explicitly address it that way too. The session as a whole gives you the space to reflect together and get to know each other well.

Interaction

Empathy and expectation management

The dialogue supported by the Co-Design Canvas and the cards has a so-called semi-structured nature. There is a sort of fixed starting point – the problematic context – but the order in which the cards are used can be determined according to their importance and personal insight. Cards may also be utilized side by side, depending on the interaction of the stakeholders. There is nothing wrong with that, but it requires extra attention by the facilitator and all stakeholders. The primary goal is a constructive dialogue in which everyone has a say, leading to mutual understanding, good expectation management and constructive collaboration.

Conclusion

Reflection in and on action

The Canvas is a tool to facilitate and structure a dialogue and co-design process, but it should not put you in a 'straitjacket' or restricting any freedom of moving in different directions. If there is disagreement on certain aspects (e.g., the results or the co-design focus), you can also use the Canvas to map it out. As such, there can be multiple questions and results on the Canvas as an outcome. A co-design process takes time, and the first session needs to be followed up; it is an iterative process, after all. Make clear agreements with all those involved regarding the subsequent steps and sessions and the communication involved. It is important to take time to reflect in and on action: during the process (in action) and afterwards (on action).

Possible CO-DESIGN CANVAS routes

To provide a good departure point for novices, advanced and experts in co-design, I below define 3 possible routes how to go through the Canvas in time.

For each route, always:

- Explore the Co-Design Canvas, its 8 cards and read the Manual as preparation
- Set up a co-design session with stakeholders lasting at least 2 hours
- Think of a good learning setting with help of the settings card

Route 1: novice

- Address the problematic situation and the complex challenge at stake supported by the context card
- Use the stakeholder card and discuss everyone's interests, knowledge and power
- Who do you miss?
- What are your insights now? Do they influence the context and can you elaborate on the purpose card?
- Plan a new session to discuss context and purpose in depth

Route 2: advanced

- Address shortly the problematic situation and the complex challenge at stake supported by the context card
- Address the possible joint purpose, aspired impact and concrete results supported by the three cards
- Use the stakeholder card and discuss everyone's interests, knowledge and power
- Relate your insights to the context, purpose, impact and result cards outcomes earlier
- Plan a new session to proceed with the focus, setting and activities cards in depth

Route 3: expert

- Address shortly the problematic situation and the complex challenge at stake supported by the context card
- Build a first boundary object together in the activities card
- Use the stakeholder card and discuss everyone's interests, knowledge and power regarding this boundary object
- Relate your insights to the context, purpose, impact and result cards outcomes earlier
- Define a co-design purpose and plan new (parallel) sessions to proceed with activities in specific settings

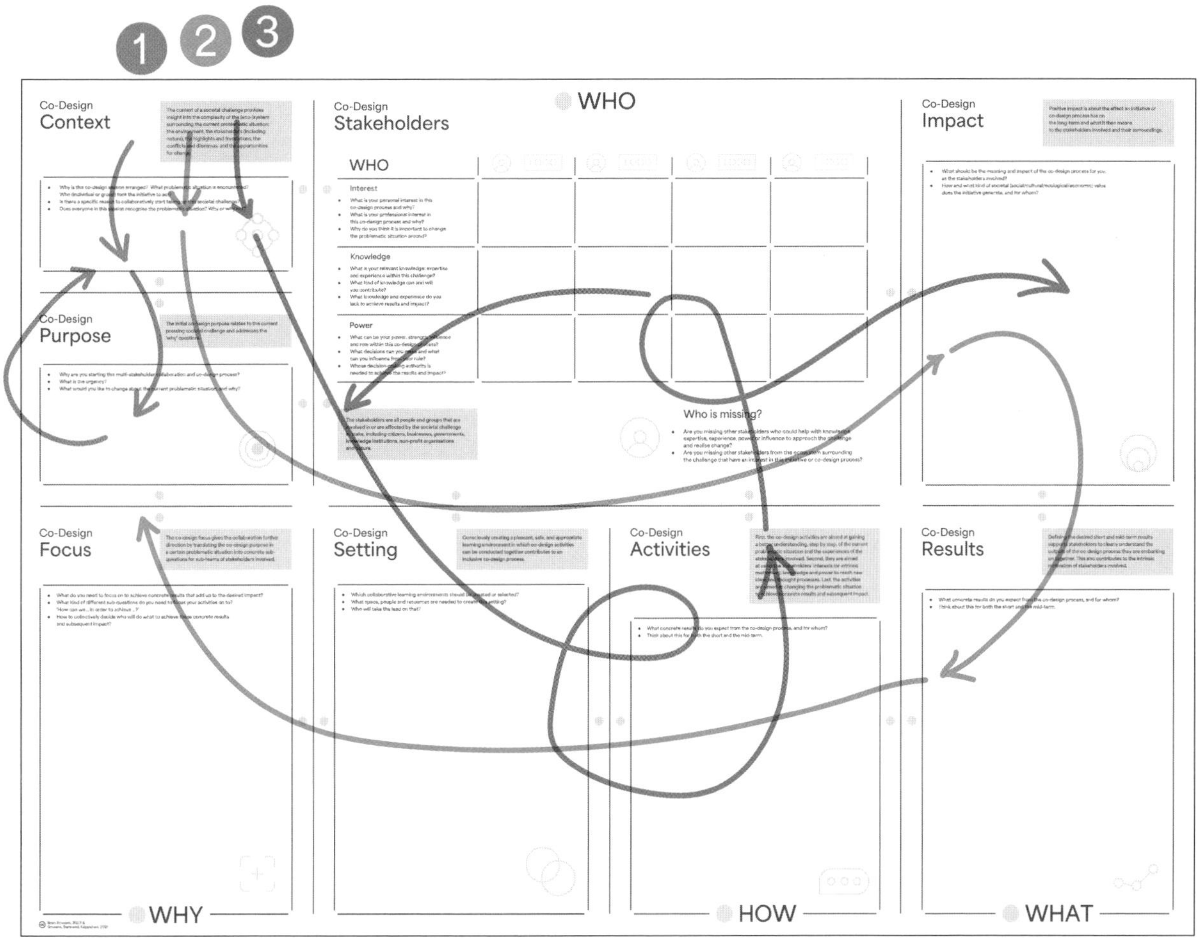

Figure 6: Co-Design Canvas routes

The 8 CO-DESIGN CANVAS cards

On the following pages you will
find all the Canvas cards

Co-Design
Context

The context of a societal challenge provides insight into the complexity of the (eco-)system surrounding the current problematic situation: the environment, the stakeholders (including nature), the highlights and frustrations, the conflicts and dilemmas, and the opportunities for change.

- Why is this co-design session arranged? What problematic situation is encountered? Who (individual or group) took the initiative to act?
- Is there a specific reason to collaboratively start taking up this societal challenge?
- Does everyone in this session recognise the problematic situation? Why or why not?

Co-Design
Context

The initiator(s) or facilitator(s) of the co-design session explain why a particular societal challenge requires change. The question to the other stakeholders present is whether they recognise the challenges in their joint context.

Does the challenge affect an entire ecosystem (e.g., the street, the neighbourhood, the municipality or even the entire country), specific groups (teams, organisations, networks) and/or individuals and the stakeholders them-selves? Is the challenge related to one or more other initiatives or projects?

Tools

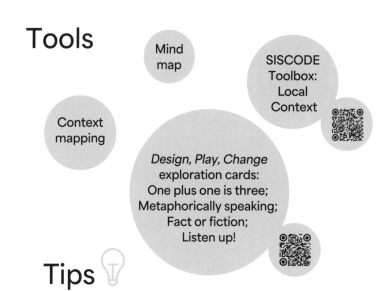

Mind map

SISCODE Toolbox: Local Context

Context mapping

Design, Play, Change exploration cards:
One plus one is three;
Metaphorically speaking;
Fact or fiction;
Listen up!

Tips 💡

When discussing the societal challenge and the eco-system surrounding a current problematic situation, the interests of different stakeholders and the desired impact and concrete results are often also discussed. Make sure everything said is included on the Canvas at those specific cards as well.

Co-Design
Purpose

The initial co-design purpose relates to the current pressing societal challenge and addresses the 'why' questions.

- Why are you starting this multi-stakeholder collaboration and co-design process?
- What is the urgency?
- What would you like to change about the current problematic situation, and why?

Co-Design
Purpose

What is the purpose that the involved stakeholders pursue with respect to this particular problematic context; for themselves, for their team, organisation or network and from the role they represent?

Specifying a common purpose also helps determine the desired concrete results and impact and who else should be involved to define the co-design focus.

Tools

Design, Play, Change - exploration cards

Design, Play, Change creation and synthesis cards: Future Stories; What if; Reframing

Who, what, when, where, why, how

SISCODE Toolbox: Problem Definition

5 Whys

Tips

The initial co-design purpose is the first opportunity for the initiators and stakeholders to transform a current pressing situation into an alternative desired future situation. During the co-design sessions, the co-design purpose will gradually become more defined leading to a clear co-design focus (see the co-design focus card).

Co-Design
Focus

The co-design focus gives the collaboration further direction by translating the co-design purpose in a certain problematic situation into concrete sub-questions for sub-teams of stakeholders involved.

- What do you need to focus on to achieve concrete results that add up to the desired impact?
- What kind of different sub-questions do you need to focus your activities on to?
  'How can we... in order to achieve ...?'
- How to collectively decide who will do what to achieve these concrete results
  and subsequent impact?

Co-Design
Focus

Once the co-design purpose, concrete results and impact have been discussed, along with who will participate how, when and why, it is time to examine the co-design focus to further clarify and detail the initiative.

This is where you define the question or sub-questions you want to explore together in the coming co-design process; i.e., the questions for which you want to seek and find design opportunities that will lead to final concrete sub-results and aspired impact.

When the stakeholders involved provide a greater variety of knowledge (expertise and experience) than the initiators expected at the start of the process, the co-design focus will be more distinct from the initial co-design purpose.

The co-design focus also depends on the concrete results and impact that the coalition aims for and agrees upon.

Tools

Shared decision making

Design, Play, Change synthesis cards: Reframing; Envisioning; Conclusions

Reframe the questions

Tips 💡

A well-defined 'How can we... in order to...?' question gives focus, not by starting from a problem but by looking for new possibilities and opportunities within the outlined context and stakeholders' aspirations.

Co-Design
Stakeholders

 **WHO**

WHO

	 LOGO	LOGO	LOGO	LOGO

Interest
- What is your personal interest in this co-design process and why?
- What is your professional interest in this co-design process and why?
- Why do you think it is important to change the problematic situation around?

Knowledge
- What is your relevant knowledge: expertise and experience within this challenge?
- What kind of knowledge can and will you contribute?
- What knowledge and experience do you lack to achieve results and impact?

Power
- What can be your power, strength, influence and role within this co-design process?
- What decisions can you make and what can you influence from your role?
- Whose decision-making authority is needed to achieve the results and impact?

The stakeholders are all people and groups that are involved in or are affected by the societal challenge at stake, including citizens, businesses, governments, knowledge institutions, non-profit organisations and nature.

Who is missing?
- Are you missing other stakeholders who could help with knowledge, expertise, experience, power or influence to approach the challenge and realise change?
- Are you missing other stakeholders from the ecosystem surrounding the challenge that have an interest in this initiative or co-design process?

Co-Design
Stakeholders

● WHO

The stakeholders are all people and groups that are involved in or are affected by the societal challenge at stake. They can come from different spheres of life, disciplines, domains and communities of practice. Think of including or representing citizens, business professionals, governmental officials, volunteers and nature. They can be present at the co-design session or not.

Their interests (similarities and differences), knowledge (experience and expertise), and power (authority, roles, influence) are important in a co-design process. In other words, we want to find out what everyone can or cannot contribute and what is important to everyone. In co-design processes, you want everyone's voice to be heard and if possible included. However, there are always differences in interests, knowledge, role, social and organisational background, etc.

In the matrix on this card, the rows represent the relevant sub-decisions and the columns represent the individual persons and collective, or collectives. You can think along the lines here of the differences between the spheres of life and the layers of teams-organisations-coalitions or streets-neighbourhoods-cities-countries.

Who?

Which people, groups and non-humans -in short which perspectives- are part of the problematic situation? This could be governments, companies, knowledge institutions, non-profit organisations, residents, citizens, visitors, even nature etc. Name them here and, if applicable, distinguish between individuals and groups.

Who are we missing?

Depending on the context, the invitation, the urgency, etc., it is possible that -particularly at the first session- not everyone with an interest in the initiative will be present. You may also need other stakeholders' knowledge or power to achieve a certain result or impact.

Knowledge

Who among the stakeholders has what relevant knowledge? This includes expertise in setting up a co-design process and creating a design or intervention, and practical knowledge of and experience with and from the challenge at hand.

Interests

Who has which interests and why? Interests can vary widely, are latent and not always clear. Various unspoken interests can complicate and frustrate the process. Think of how you can include all the interests from the very beginning. They can also affect your role as a stakeholder in the process. The same holds for personal motives and concerns. Understanding and empathy for each other's perception and experiences also play an important role. Be open, honest and respectful.

Power

Who among the stakeholders has what power, strength, influence or role? There is often a power imbalance in collaboration processes, though it is not always explicitly mentioned and experienced. Power or influence is not only determined by a person's position or the organisation they represent; sometimes it is about financial power or authority, but power can also stem from someone's network, knowledge, skills or personality. Failure to explicitly acknowledge or account for existing power relations and associated interests can lead to frustration among those involved. To collaborate respectfully and on equal footing, clarifying and expressing these differences is crucial, as is the space to share or not share power. It is important to create space to question existing power relations, discuss (in)equalities and take a step back if necessary.

Tools

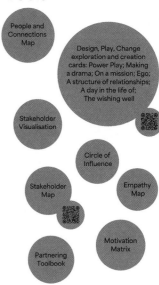

People and Connections Map

Design, Play, Change exploration and creation cards: Power Play; Making a drama; On a mission; Ego; A structure of relationships; A day in the life of; The wishing well

Stakeholder Visualisation

Circle of Influence

Stakeholder Map

Empathy Map

Motivation Matrix

Partnering Toolbook

Tips 💡

Problems in collaborative processes often arise from tensions between stakeholders, e.g., due to power imbalance or social contingencies that evolve, and were not foreseen nor discussed beforehand. The Canvas can clarify these issues and relationships beforehand and offer stakeholders a common language to reflect in and on the process.

Who: Add photos and logos to make the overview of stakeholders come alive. Are there any important connections to be drawn?
Are there more than six individuals or groups that have an interest in or are affected by this co-design process or initiative? If so, use an extra sheet of paper. Do not let the space on the Canvas limit you.

Interests: Include quotes and visualisations, and establish the similarities and differences between people and organisations.

Knowledge: Make an overview of the necessary knowledge and document who has what knowledge, why it can be useful and what knowledge is still lacking.

Power: Outline the ecosystem and indicate who has which role, influence and decision-making authority.

Who are you missing: Add pictures and logos of people and groups and state why they should be involved. Discuss why they are not present now and how they can be involved in the follow-up process.

Co-Design
Results

Defining the desired short and mid-term results supports stakeholders to clearly understand the outputs of the co-design process they are embarking on together. This also contributes to the intrinsic motivation of stakeholders involved.

- What concrete results do you expect from the co-design process, and for whom?
- Think about this for both the short and the mid-term.

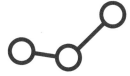

Co-Design
Results

Tools

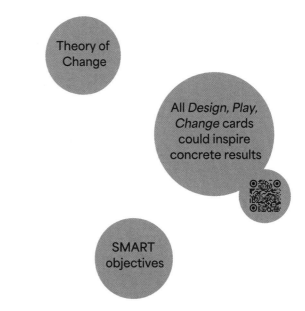

Theory of Change

All *Design, Play, Change* cards could inspire concrete results

SMART objectives

It is important to define immediate concrete results to establish what each stakeholder involved expects from the cooperation and to manage these expectations.

Collectively defining the desired short-term results and their longer term significance for people (see also the impact card) not only benefits stakeholders' intrinsic motivation, but is also key to assessing the success of a co-design process later on.

By formulating the desired results at the start of the co-design process, you can better determine which insights, ideas and resources are needed and who can do what.

A result can be a plan, an idea direction, a work process, an experience, a product, a service, etc.

Tips

The results are influenced by the co-design setting in which co-design activities are carried out, by the type of activities, and by which stakeholders participate in what activities. Be aware of this at all times.

Co-Design
Impact

Positive impact is about the effect an initiative or co-design process has on
the long-term and what it then means
to the stakeholders involved and their surroundings.

- What should be the meaning and impact of the co-design process for you, as the stakeholders involved?
- How and what kind of societal (social/cultural/ecological/economic) value does the initiative generate, and for whom?

Co-Design

Impact

Tools

Positive impact stems from both the concrete results and the process; it is about the meaning and the effect of both of them on the people involved.

Impact can develop as early as the kick-off meeting. It could mean a different mindset, understanding and empathy for each other, a change in behaviour, or a change in culture or future perspective.

Design, Play, Change creation, evaluation and synthesis cards: Future dreams; What if; Provocative Prototypes; Detectives; Envisioning

Theory of change

Social Return on Investment

Tips

The interests, knowledge and power of the stakeholders involved affect the co-design impact. Be aware of this at all times.

Co-Design
Activities

First, the co-design activities are aimed at gaining a better understanding, step by step, of the current problematic situation and the experiences of the stakeholders involved. Second, they are aimed at using the stakeholders' interests (or intrinsic motivation), knowledge and power to reach new ideas and thought processes. Last, the activities are aimed at changing the problematic situation to achieve concrete results and subsequent impact.

- What co-design process and associated activities will you (need to) develop, set up and carry out together (how long, in what order, simultaneously or in sequence, etc.)?
- What resources and people do you need for that?
- When do you make what decision or reach a conclusion?

Co-Design
Activities

The type of co-design activities that will be selected and developed, in what order, and how they will be conducted depends on the time taken for the co-design process, the focus, the context and the stakeholders involved.

In any case, it involves an iterative co-design process of divergence and convergence leading to initial ideas, clearly defined concepts, prototypes, testing and a conclusion.

A co-design process will require multiple sessions and activities, and you should consider an evaluation and test with the community and stakeholders.

Moreover, it is important to start with the most appealing and most relevant 'How can we... in order to...?' questions, as previously defined in the co-design focus card. This can be the start of a small co-design project in a sub-team which is part of a bigger portfolio of projects. Then, starting from this question, select or develop appropriate methods and materials (settings) to obtain initial design opportunities and ideas to achieve first results that add up to aspired impact.

Tools

Define the process SISCODE

Make (paper) prototypes, improvise, test, evaluate and conclude

Develop and use co-design tools, boundary objects and convivial tools

Generate and select idea directions and concepts

All *Design, Play, Change* exploration, creation and evaluation cards, and page 76 of the book

Tips

When developing your co-design process, consider the methods and materials you intend to or can use, and in what order, to answer the 'How can we... in order to...?' question or questions creatively. A (social) designer can also support you here.

Co-Design
Setting

Consciously creating a pleasant, safe, and appropriate learning environment in which co-design activities can be conducted together contributes to an inclusive co-design process.

- Which collaborative learning environments should be created or selected?
- What space, people and resources are needed to create this setting?
- Who will take the lead on that?

Co-Design
Setting

The learning environments in which the co-design activities will be conducted can be selected in situ (in context) or not (more neutral). This largely depends on the co-design focus, the context and the stakeholders involved.

Also consider who will be facilitating the activities, who you will be inviting and how, whether there will be in parallel sessions in sub-teams or a plenary session, in a place accessible to all stakeholders, whether it will take place online or offline, at what time the activities will take place, how long the process will/may take, whether refreshments and coffee or tea are needed, etc.

The resources and people needed include the budget for facilitators, the hours for those involved, as well as knowledge, expertise, experience and design materials.

The co-design focus and the diversity (in interests, knowledge and power) of the stakeholders involved affect the co-design setting and activities.

Tools

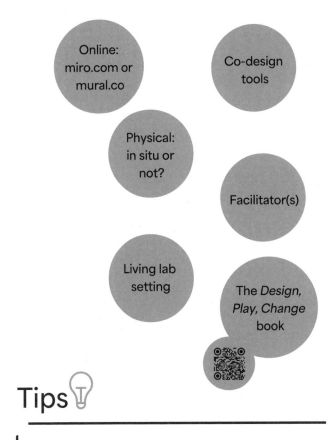

Online: miro.com or mural.co

Co-design tools

Physical: in situ or not?

Facilitator(s)

Living lab setting

The *Design, Play, Change* book

Tips

A (social) co-designer can be a good co-design process developer and facilitator. It is good to consider inclusiveness: the choice of a physical space or online environment has implications for accessibility. Does your choice exclude anyone?

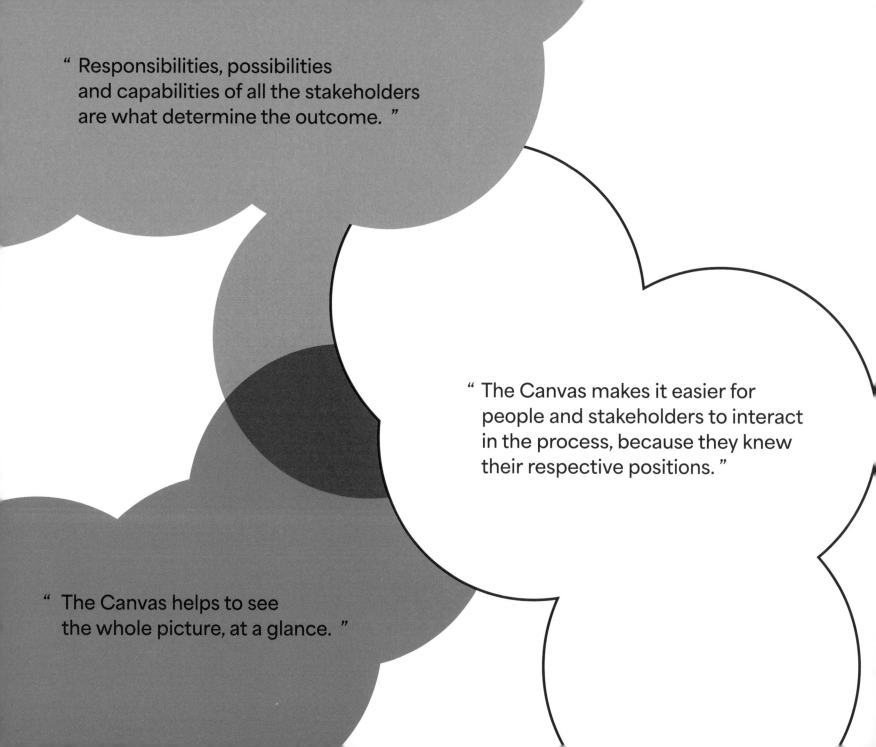

" Responsibilities, possibilities and capabilities of all the stakeholders are what determine the outcome. "

" The Canvas makes it easier for people and stakeholders to interact in the process, because they knew their respective positions. "

" The Canvas helps to see the whole picture, at a glance. "

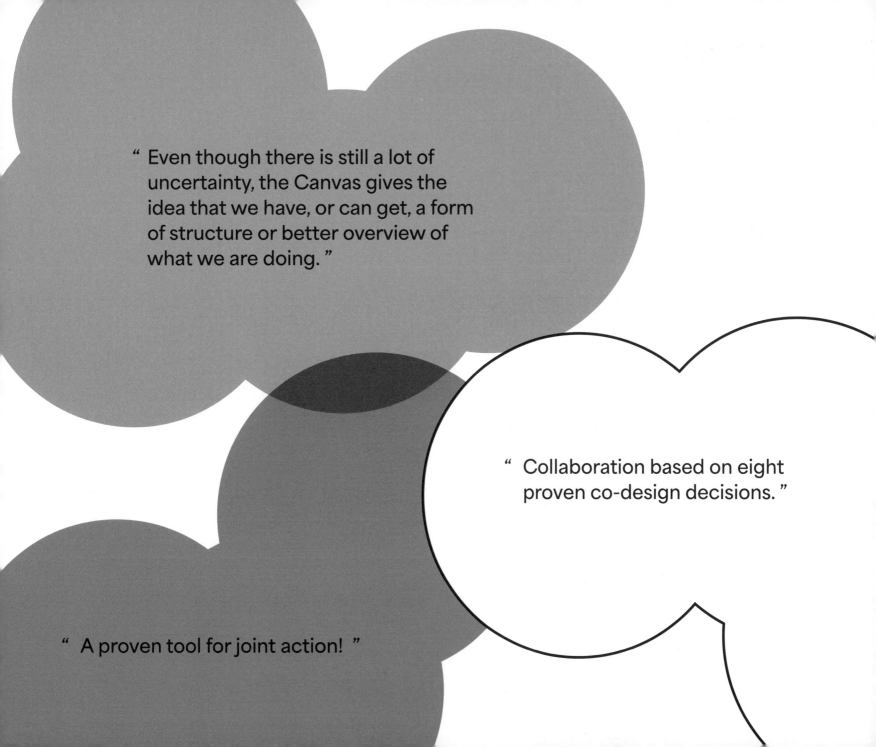

" Even though there is still a lot of uncertainty, the Canvas gives the idea that we have, or can get, a form of structure or better overview of what we are doing. "

" Collaboration based on eight proven co-design decisions. "

" A proven tool for joint action! "

5

The CANVAS in the wild

In this chapter, you can read the five duo interviews with the people of various backgrounds that developed, studied, worked and have been working with the Co-Design Canvas the past two years.

They involve Co-Design Canvas developers, practitioners, change makers, researchers, and education professionals. Their reflections, experiences and stories might bring you some more inspiration and contextualisation before you start working with the Co-Design Canvas yourself. Due to the interviewees' different backgrounds, you might recognise your own stance in change and co-design processes. Their enthusiasm, experiences, tips, tricks, and struggles might illustrate that working together towards change is by no means always easy and demands stamina and staying power. Between the lines, you can also read about the lessons learned, positive effects, results and impacts of using the Canvas in the wild.

The CO-DESIGN CANVAS is:
a conversation tool
a generative tool
a learning tool
a repair tool
a selection tool
a social contract
an intentional tool
a deliberate co-design tool

What was amusing when looking at the interview transcriptions were the terms used by the technology to refer to the Co-Design Canvas. I would like to share a little of this source of amusement with you. For the transcription technology, the new term Co-Design Canvas was interpreted as follows: the cocaine fest; the goldfish and camper; the coke-creative canvas; the code-share campus; the coalition caravan; the co-design combat; ...

Bio Anja Köppchen

Anja has a background in human geography. Co-design processes have played a recurring role for her in several (research) projects since she defended her PhD thesis at Radboud University in 2014. From 2015-2021, Anja co-developed and coordinated the design labs of Cube design museum. Her focus was on coaching students and facilitating and encouraging co-creation between various stakeholders, including museum visitors. As part of the SISCODE project, Anja was responsible for coordinating a co-creation journey with local citizens and policymakers, resulting in the Co-Design Canvas. The contexts of other projects vary. They include co-creation between textile designers and producers, circular design strategies, business developers and scientists valorising waste streams and safety challenges in the chemistry sector. From her love of nature and a growing concern about the loss of biodiversity, she aspires to strengthen the role of non-human actors in her current and future work.

Bio Gène Bertrand

Gène is the head of programme and development at Museumplein Limburg. He has a background in culture, media, education and PR/marketing, and has been involved in the setup and development of Cube's co-creation and co-design labs in recent years. Throughout his 40-plus years' of experience, Gène has been involved in setting up and developing Museumplein Limburg's three museums. He was a co-curator of several exhibition projects, including 'Brain', developed in cooperation with colleagues from Copenhagen and Göteborg. One of his recent projects was the 'Nature' exhibition in collaboration with Cooper Hewitt, Smithsonian Design Museum in New York. He is responsible for international cooperation and is involved in designing and implementing many European projects and partnerships. His approach and working methods focus on co-design working with partners to create projects and content aimed at visitor participation.

The CO-DESIGN CANVAS co-developers

Wina
How did the Co-Design Canvas come about?

Anja

One thing comes up now when I think of how our SISCODE project actually started. We - as a design museum - stepped into a project context in which a lot had already happened or a lot was already going on. We wanted to support the participation processes of citizens and policy makers in a shrinking village. But, we did not know the people living there, nor what was going on. We did have an overall idea of wanting to do something with the main societal challenges in this southern region of the Netherlands. But the purpose of the project was still very open. When we stepped into this context, we needed to understand it. We were not only looking for a deliverable that could help citizens and policymakers alike, we were also exploring how we could find a way to take the next step in their collaboration.

Gène

I think this is quite an important point you make. Before the Canvas even existed, we already had a lot of experience in co-creation. Yet, we mostly used Design-Thinking and Service-Design methods to develop product concepts or services. Now, our challenge was more focused on social design. Which was more challenging for us than the other methodologies I just mentioned. And that is why we needed your expertise Wina, as well as some sort of tool that could help us in this. In groups, there are always differences in backgrounds and capabilities. Moreover, what is always quite

important in my opinion is managing expectations in a group. These were two sides of a coin that always played a role in our co-creation sessions. With different people at the table, each with different backgrounds, different responsibilities, and so on. It was always important to get clarity on what everybody's position in the co-design process was to be. For me, the SISCODE project was a very interesting development journey that we made together and which culminated in the development of t his great Co-Design Canvas.

Wina
How would you describe the development journey that we embarked on together?

Gène

It was like every co-creation journey that we know to be a process of trial, error and, success. When we started this journey, we did not have a clear idea of what the outcome would be. The idea of a canvas developed during the journey. We were part of a European Horizon 2020 project and the challenge we faced was that of an ageing society. It was therefore a very broad topic, which is quite normal in design processes. During that journey, it became more and more clear what we needed to develop, based on our experiences during the process. There is a strong case in development processes like these for you to develop something that is based around the needs of the people around the table. And in my opinion this Co-Design Canvas journey was quite a powerful journey with a powerful result.

Anja

Throughout the process, we learned that a more complicated question was being asked by the ageing community and that our different stakeholders needed a new process to work together. At some point, it was no longer about the need for a new building or service for elderly people, or about the specific challenges within this village. No, it was more about how we could support the collaborative process of the policymakers and citizens working on the relevant societal challenges.

Wina

Indeed, together we found that it was not the ideas that were missing in this ageing village. The challenge had more to do with the non-connection and the relationships between the citizens and policymakers. What was necessary to really get started was to establish ownership of a societal challenge by all the relevant stakeholders.

Gène

One of the things we experienced is that it is quite difficult to get everybody reading off the same page. When you start with a co-design process there are different problems. You need to make sure that everybody discusses things in the same context, gets to a common purpose or change objective, with the same focus, and so on. I think this project was quite good, because we worked with real people, who have real issues. It resulted in a concrete Co-Design Canvas tool which is very usable. It also means that the resulting Canvas is not just based on theory; it is grounded in the real world.

Wina

How would you describe the Co-Design Canvas?

Gène

The Canvas is a tool that brings people together and gets them on the same level, which is a good starting point for a co-design process. For example, it seems obvious for us all when I tell somebody 'I see a blue sky'. But another person who looks up could have a completely different interpretation. I experience this quite often. I might, for example, be explaining about what I experienced in a meeting. Someone else then relates their experience in that very same meeting, but it turns out to be a completely different story than what I myself experienced. I think the Co-Design Canvas helps provide a common ground. A common ground from which to start, that is what the co-design process consists of. And it is quite important to establish this, otherwise you will lose a lot of time and effort in making it clear what you mean, where you want to start and what you want to reach or achieve.

'I think the Co-Design Canvas helps provide a common ground'

Anja

We have already used the Canvas many times, and in different contexts. For me the Canvas is definitely a tool that supports the co-design process in several ways. Indeed, as Gène said, to start the process, but also throughout the process. I also agree that the Canvas helps people find common ground, to almost literally, read off the same page. The Canvas helps to explicate where everybody stands, what everybody brings to the table, but also who and what is missing. So, in that way the Canvas is also a conversation tool.

Gène

The Co-Design Canvas also helps to make people realise what is important in a co-design process, what kind of steps need to be taken and what kind of angles or perspectives the process needs. When we started this process and talked to the people from the municipality and from all kinds of other organisations, I think 80 per cent of them did not realise what kind of topics and elements are important in a co-design session. But after using the Canvas, they appreciated the added value of co-design. In a co-design process, it is not just about listening to what somebody says. The Canvas helps to make the stakeholders aware about what is necessary for a good co-design process to evolve.

> ### *Wina*
> *In a way, I hear you say that the Co-Design Canvas creates awareness of the conditions you need to start a co-design process.*

Gène

More than that, the Canvas creates awareness of your own position in the co-design process and in the group that you are collaborating with. What we learned is that the policy makers realised what their power was, but at the same moment they also realised that other peopl e in the group, people with different backgrounds and responsibilities, also have some sort of power. It is not only what we always seem to think: the person in charge of the money has the power. No, it is different. The Canvas is more subtle than that. I think that that is one of the good things we realised in this process. That it is easier for people and stakeholders to interact in the process, because they knew their respective positions. And I think the Co-Design Canvas helps to clarify these different stakeholder positions.

Anja

I think that is very important. At that point the co-design process is no longer just an abstract process with rules or something; it becomes a process in which everyone has a different position and plays a different role. Realising that for yourself, as well as in relation to the others involved in the co-design process, that is very important.

Gène

The Canvas makes everybody aware that success depends on their active participation. Everybody who is involved in this canvas process influences the outcome. Which gives responsibility, as well as status in the process. Status is important, because when you start a co-design process not everybody realises what their own position is in that process. Some people overstate their status while some people underestimate it. Everybody plays a certain role in the co-design process and they are all more or less at the same level.

Anja

I do not know if I would agree that everybody is more or less at the same level. Yes, they all play a role, but I am not sure if they are all necessarily equal. However, it is certainly a good thing that everyone is aware of where they stand.

Gène

I mean equal in the sense that everyone can play a certain role in a certain part or moment of the co-design process. That their influence in that part of the process is important. Stakeholders are only equal in the sense that they influence the complete co-design process. That is actually what I meant. Not equal in the other sense, because that would not be the idea. The responsibilities, possibilities and capabilities of all the stakeholders are what determine the outcome. The equality is in the influence that it has on the co-design process. If you are aware of what your role is in the co-design process, I think there are two sides. On one hand, you will be aware that you have a certain responsibility to the other partners, because if you do not do what is expected of you it will influence the outcome. So, that is not a good idea. On the other hand, because you are addressing all the co-design elements and cards that are on the Canvas, you will better understand the others. You will be able to see the situation from different sides and perspectives. Take the municipality official for instance, what is his or her responsibility in this position? Citizens often have little idea of what municipality officials have to do. Conversely, the distance between politicians and citizens is also increasing. In my opinion, people and stakeholders do not normally take enough time to look over the fence and see the situation on the other side. The Co-Design Canvas forces stakeholders to look over their fences.

Anja

It would be too easy to say that the Co-Design Canvas makes people more empathic. The Canvas is just a tool. But by taking the time to make explicit what everyone is bringing to the table, how everyone works and what their respective positions are, it will at least help to provide a better understanding of each other. Some feedback I received from the people we worked with is that by just taking the time to discuss all these co-design aspects and cards it already helps. Often, you do not even discuss why stakeholders are present in a co-design session, what kind of knowledge they bring to the table and what their power relations are. Taking the time to discuss this together will help get a better understanding of each other. That, in itself, will help to develop empathy for one another.

Gene

The cards and the Canvas force stakeholders to pay attention to the different co-design elements.

> ### *Wina*
> **Are you still using the Co-Design Canvas?**

Gène

I use parts of the Canvas, not the complete version. Since the SISCODE project, social innovation or societal design have not been on our museums' agenda. That said, the Canvas made me aware that in some projects or processes, we can certainly use parts of it. The Canvas prompts me as to where I should focus on when starting up a co-design process. Every six months, for example, we work with a few students from high schools. They work in our discovery museum for three or four days a week. Typically, they will have to create something, a project about sustainability, for example, or robots or artificial intelligence. We always start with a design-introduction workshop. This is because we want to encourage them not to just launch into the first good idea that springs to mind, but to learn to work together in finding a design opportunity. Then, we use parts of the Canvas to address certain topics. Empathy towards others in the group and towards stakeholders is quite important. In a complete co-design process I think that all the cards of the Canvas will be addressed, but not all at the same moment. Let me put this another way: it is not the outcome that is important, it is the students' education process. Clearly, we can use the Canvas in different ways. We can use it three or four times, for example, but always by using different sub questions which are relevant to that part of the design process for the students. Depending on the people in the group, their backgrounds and their motivations, I will give the students different cards. In this way, each group or team will actually take different routes through the Canvas. If, at the end of the process, I see collaboration between students who normally would not work together, I conclude that something good has happened. For students, a co-design project should be a rich learning environment. These co-design elements in the Canvas cards are things they would normally never even think about when carrying out a school project.

Wina
Are you saying that you have kind of internalised the Co-Design Canvas and its cards, and in so doing you are able to use it more creatively in practice?

Gène
Yes, but so far it is much more internalised in my own way of working than in the institution's.

Anja
That is interesting, because it means that you are not literally using the Canvas as such.

Gène
That is something I do not believe in. I would not advocate literally using a canvas like this because every situation is different. And given that every question more or less differs in detail, I think the strongest canvas is one in which I can adapt the question, challenge or problematic situation. This flexibility is certainly a strong feature of the Co-Design Canvas.

Wina
This brings me to another question. Do you think that this way of working on the Canvas' elements could replace current change- or design-processes?

Gene
I do not know whether the Canvas could replace a design process. For me, design processes make people aware of ways you can approach a design challenge. Yet these existing, more traditional, processes do not take into account the differences between the people who are part of the challenge and the co-design process itself: the design team and the stakeholders. And exactly there lies the strength of the Co-Design Canvas: it is much more focused on the participants and their relationships than on the design process itself. I think it can work both ways. Personally, I need the 'Double Diamond' process to make it clear to students what our design process is, for example, why we want them to collect a diversity of ideas and why they have to bring these together in only three concepts. Afterwards, I take a closer look at the participants or students at the table and make them also aware of what their role is in that 'Double Diamond' process. This makes me think that the Canvas is a more generative tool.

Anja
I agree with what Gène says: that you always adapt your process to the specific problematic situation and that all these different processes offer something. The Co-Design Canvas does not dictate the creative process itself. It offers some tools. But there are so many tools and it depends what works in a specific situation. These other kind of processes help more in that part: to create something. I do not know whether the Canvas could replace design processes; I doubt that it could. However, the Canvas and other design or change processes can certainly build on and complement one another.

Gène

I just realised something. Yesterday, I was in a meeting for a yet-to-be-developed new high school, based on the ideas of Martin Buber and it underscored the importance of dialogue between people. The premise of the school is that the children will follow lessons in a central location during the mornings on subjects such as mathematics, reading and writing, then the afternoons will be spent having lessons in the city with partners, such as a music school, the theatre or the zoo. Now what I realised is that the representatives of these different partner organisations are totally different people with different approaches, perspectives, backgrounds and responsibilities. I think that it might be a good idea to use the Co-Design Canvas in this situation. This is because, generally speaking, people are more or less stuck in their normal thinking patterns. Teachers have typically been giving lessons for 10 or 15 years already. Education innovation experts are stuck in their innovation processes. And the people from the different institutes in how their institutes work. There is a lot of uncertainty and questions in developing a new school. I think that this could be a good new situation to work with this Canvas.

> ### Wina
> *That raises the very interesting question of how we can keep the Canvas top of mind. It is always a challenge with tools like these because they tend to slip into the background as you revert to your normal working routine.*

Gène

The only way to keep the Canvas topical is to spread the word and make sure it is used as often as possible. That will take some work, because the Co-Design Canvas is not easy. To appreciate its value, you have to understand certain basics about co-design and design processes. You have to go through the co-design process with the Canvas before it becomes clear what its value is. In a way, this is also a communication challenge, because just telling people to use it will not be enough. The only way for it to work is to have experts use it, or to have people work with it so that they experience the Canvas first-hand and see the value of using it.

Anja

That reminds me. I used the Co-Design Canvas in the Interreg project at the Discovery Museum. It was with quite a big group of stakeholders in a value chain in the healthcare sector. These stakeholders ranged from the supplier of raw materials to the producer of medical devices and from healthcare institutions to the waste processor. They all came to the Netherlands from various different countries. Using the Canvas was a very good experience for them, in the sense that it gave them a better understanding of each other's roles. And they took the time to see what everyone else does in the supply chain, with the common goal of becoming more circular. But while they all very much appreciated the process, they also conceded that they would not be able to do it without good facilitation and they would not do it again afterwards if it is not coordinated by us.

> ### Wina
> *So do we need to set up a Co-Design Canvas 'school' or 'community of practice'?*

Gène

Yes!

Design, Play, Change

Anja

I do not know. In the example I cited, the producer of medical devices initiated the value-chain meeting. Were he to get some training, he would be able to conduct the Canvas himself, but that still implies that there must be one person or organisation who has to be the initiator. This particular company certainly has this ambition and was therefore willing to assume the responsibility. But I feel that with most companies it is not something that comes naturally and I do not know how to encourage them to assume this responsibility.

> ### Wina
> *Ownership is a common problem, which naturally brings me to my next question, about tips and tricks. Do you have any?*

Gène

Changing the system is also something that applies here. What I have realised, and find quite frustrating, is that people are afraid of uncertainty. My discussions on co-design processes and projects are mainly about the 'game'. People often ask: 'What do you want from us?' or 'What is our role?' for example. And I think: 'Wait, that is not important at the moment'. They need to dive into the process *with* me, see what is happening and establish what is needed. But that is still a very big ask for many people. The Co-Design Canvas helps to facilitate the process. But what can we do when people or stakeholders will not even consider letting go of their normal routine and diving into a co-design process? That is the first stage. Before that, they will not even realise how the Canvas can add value. But I feel I need to do a lot of missionary work to convince them. They are always so dependent on their own methodology and current way of working. It is sometimes quite hard to find people with the open-mindedness to change what they always do. This is certainly the case in education and schools. I find that very worrying.

Anja

What is nice, and sort of 'easy', about the Canvas is that it seems to give a certain structure. And everyone appears to be open enough to recognise that structure. It is not like: 'Oh help, are we going to play with Lego?'. What often happens when you introduce creative design tools to a building process like Lego for example, or even scarier stuff, is that for many managers it is not really what they consider normal. In a way, the Co Design Canvas comprises simple boxes with questions. And in that way it is quite similar to what many people already do when they try to structure things. It feels more acceptable and easier to work with. And it does not matter what your background is, you will be able to understand what you are doing. Even though there is still a lot of uncertainty, the Canvas gives the idea that we have, or can get, a form of structure or better overview of what we are doing. That, I think, is a clear strength of the Canvas.

Gène

But that is only the beginning. When it comes to using the Canvas, expectation management is also quite important.

Anja

That is indeed a big issue that I also struggle with. I think it relates to the question of how to keep it topical or not make it a mere box-ticking exercise. How can the Canvas really help throughout the process and not just in starting something up?

Gène

You have to convince participants that the outcome of the process will be better if they use the Canvas than it would be if they just start with their basic ideas and then apply normal procedures. And that will always be a problem.

> ## Wina
> *And finally, did I forget to ask you anything?*

Anja

How about impact? Using the Canvas really makes, or at least can, make an impact. But it is really hard to keep track of that impact because it would take a lot of time to look into what is going on in different projects and what exactly you should be looking for. Anyway, how can you actually measure what is going on?

Gène

On the other hand, if the Canvas were to be used in the whole school for students carrying out projects in different departments, you would see that impact evolving. When I think back to our design labs, I remember that the first thing we had to do was to take students out of the mindset of what they learned in school. The Canvas could be an excellent tool in facilitating that process. If you have the opportunity to work with a new group of students every year, it could constitute a good research environment in which carrying out a study into the use of the Canvas. So that it can be further developed.

Anja

I agree. If we still had the design labs in the museum, I would start using the Co-Design Canvas, which before this, of course, we did not have. Before, every time a new group of students arrived, we adjusted the design process based upon what we learned from the last time. But it was building the team that took most of the time and effort and the Co-Design Canvas could have been supportive in this respect.

SISCODE

The Co-Design Canvas originated in the co-design journey made by Cube design museum together with inhabitants of Ransdaal and the municipality of Voerendaal as part of the SISCODE project. The content and working method was developed in cooperation with and facilitated by Wina Smeenk and is partly based on the *Design Choices Framework for Co-creation Projects (Lee et al., 2018)..* This framework provides insight into the variables and uncertainties that can influence a co-design process, as well as their interdependencies.

SISCODE was a 3-year Horizon 2020 project, involving 18 partners from 13 countries, led by Politecnico di Milano. It aimed to provide insights into the power and possibilities of co-design for political decision-making and reduce the gap from idea generation to actual policy implementation. How might we approach complex policy issues in a different, innovative way, developing policies through co-design and co-creation with citizens and other stakeholders instead of from the top down? Effecting change on a large scale requires starting small. Ten different co-design labs (from Dublin to Paris and from Copenhagen to Krakow) experimented with co-creation and co-design methods applied to a local challenge. Cube design museum was one of those labs.

SISCODE toolbox

Bio Ko Koens

Ko is Professor of New Urban Tourism at Inholland University of Applied Sciences, as well as being active in Breda University of Applied Sciences and the University of Johannesburg. He has been involved in sustainable tourism for nearly twenty years, focusing on topics such as new urban tourism, overtourism, city hospitality and tourism of inequalities (slum tourism). His work is characterised by its transdisciplinary nature, incorporating elements from urban planning, sociology, social psychology, environmental sciences and, increasingly, design studies. More recently, Ko founded the international Expertise Network Sustainable New Urban Tourism which seeks to bring together academics of different backgrounds, with industry, government, and NGO stakeholders to make cities better places for all to live in and to visit. Part of ENSUT's work is performed in living labs. Ko is lab lead for the Urban Leisure and Tourism Lab Rotterdam.

Bio Claudia Mayer

Claudia is a researcher at the Societal Impact Design Research group and a lecturer in International Creative Business at Inholland University of Applied Sciences. With a Business Administration master's degree from the University of Innsbruck (Austria), she brings to the table 15-plus years of cross-sector experience in Europe and Asia. Claudia's research involves innovative teaching methodologies for experiential living labs, with a focus on the Co-Design Canvas, Stakeholder Mapping, and Multiple Perspectives. She participates in collaborative research initiatives, engaging with both internal and external stakeholders. As an educator, she imparts Design Thinking and media-production knowledge to undergraduates. Aside from academia, Claudia runs a consultancy for design SMEs, guiding and enhancing their marketing and sales strategies. Her collaborative process leverages smart technology platforms and AI-based business tools.

The CO-DESIGN CANVAS in tourism

Wina

How did you come into contact with the Co-Design Canvas?

Claudia

It was through my work at the Urban and Leisure and Tourism Lab in Amsterdam two years ago. You, Wina, gave a workshop introducing the Canvas to the students and I was working as a learning coach or learning director.

Ko

It was probably not long afterwards that I encountered the Canvas, when you, Wina, started your professorship, or maybe even before that. At least, when I started working with you, you introduced me to the concept of the Co-Design Canvas as something you had been developing. Initially, the Canvas was only a topic of conversation, but after about seven months I got to experience what it actually was. The Canvas represented a very interesting concept for me.

Wina

What was it about the Co-Design Canvas that appealed to you?

Ko

At the time, I was mostly acquainted with standard business canvases, which I find very one-dimensional and take economic growth as the imperative. With many other canvases, the basic assumption is all about business.

The Co-Design Canvas takes a very different approach and is more flexible. There are different ways in which you can use it and it can be used in different contexts. So for me it is much more than a 'normal' business tool. I like its flexibility and the fact that the stakeholders are at its core. For me, as a professor in tourism, stakeholder management is a key part of the Canvas. To see a tool that actually focuses on that, rather than on business or technological solutions or what you might, in a derogative sense, term as 'happy-clappy' design efforts, was very appealing.

Claudia

My perspective differs from Ko's, because in my work I am much more exposed to creative tools and methodologies. The Co-Design Canvas enriches and deepens design teaching, because it includes the co-design elements. In design, a project team is assigned to a certain challenge or assignment. The team is leading in this process, going through a number of design phases, depending on the methodology that is chosen. In traditional Stanford D-school Design Thinking, the empathise phase is the one in which the design team works on understanding the context. They mainly research the target group. It is therefore not as rich as the Co-Design Canvas, which involves all stakeholders in a particular problematic context. The Co-Design Canvas supports the view that there are more relevant people than just those in the target group. Then, in design thinking the team defines the design question, ideates and then enters the prototyping and testing phase, in which the team shows its concepts to the target group, to elicit feedback and evaluate the desirability of the concepts. So what is new in the Co-Design Canvas? The depth of not just asking: 'What are your wishes and needs?', but addressing the three Canvas stakeholder card elements, namely power, knowledge and interest. And then specifying these questions. In this respect, the Canvas goes even deeper. At the bottom of the stakeholder canvas card, for example, it asks: 'Who are we missing?', which begs the question: 'Are we really complete?'. It also invites you to think about who else might be relevant. These aspects are very appealing to me. The notion that co-design is a collaboration during the whole design process, not just in the empathy and testing phases. Given that you work together in the whole design process, the Canvas enriches both the 'co-' and the 'design'.

Wina
If you had to describe the Co-Design Canvas in a nutshell, how would you do so?

Ko
The Co-Design Canvas is a canvas, but not in the commonly accepted sense. It is a canvas that focuses on how to work together and provide clarity on what you can do together, rather than focusing only on yourself. As part of a co-design process, rather than an individual one. The Canvas actually instigates, changes and moves beyond other canvases that tell you what you should do personally. Instead, the Canvas is about what we can do.

Claudia
I like the fact that you said: 'what we can do'. I love it. I normally use 'being on the same page'. The Canvas is literally that same page. The page that makes you aligned. I know from the developers of the Canvas that it is based on

scientific research about the success factors of collaboration in co-creation projects. Moreover, the Canvas is very approachable and visual; it invites you to explore and look at the cards and its elements. I would say the Canvas is a tool that gets everyone on the same page.

Wina
And why do you think the Canvas is important for students to use?

Claudia
I will answer that from two perspectives. One is from a mindset perspective, because it triggers conversation and reflection. The sub-questions in the Canvas cards are not easily answered with a 'yes' or a 'no'. The questions are quite open and they naturally invite you to enter into some form of dialogue. It serves as a trigger to a curious mindset. To go deeper and clarify, for instance, the power element. That stimulates a team to discuss it, which is maybe not easy, or perhaps students do not automatically think about it. Yet, power is a very crucial element. One that can make or break a collaboration. The Canvas stimulates you to go deeper, explore what a certain co-design card term means and why it is important. Moreover, as a tool or process, the Canvas is visual. Almost like a game. The Canvas does not have a clear or mandatory starting and ending point, so it encourages the playful exploration of the different coloured sections and cards. This makes it more approachable for our students. We use a big printed canvas carpet of three by two metres, around and on which students can either sit or stand. Like twister. Sometimes, we use a dice to pick a card. Other times, we use clay or plasticine instead of Post-its, to playfully explore the Canvas. Sometimes, I also cover up some of the Canvas' sections or cards. Other times, I let the students

throw a ball, or ask them what was important in their last student collaboration. Their answers then activate previous knowledge and students will invariably conclude that using the Canvas is not rocket science. They have experienced all these elements, but now these elements are just clustered on a canvas. Fortunately, students are used to canvas-oriented thinking, which makes it easier to introduce the Co-Design Canvas and thus make this complex knowledge accessible. However, the Canvas is not a self-explanatory tool. You cannot simply give it to students and say: 'good luck, have fun and come back in half an hour'. We tried that. But even when we provided the Manual, students still needed more support. I have an elaborated reflection on that. The Canvas is like the Business Model Canvas or the Value Proposition Canvas. It is a tool. As a tool, the Canvas makes complex knowledge more accessible, but it still needs an open mind and requires explanation and experience to show its value. And allow for the depth that I mentioned earlier.

Ko

We too used the Canvas with the students in our Urban Leisure and Tourism lab in Rotterdam. For me, the value of the Canvas is its ability to make the key issues of co-design very clear. Claudia already mentioned power, which is something that is all-too-often ignored, either because it is seen as too difficult, too fuzzy a subject or just downright confusing. Yet, power is omnipresent. Moreover, the Canvas throws light on the large number of stakeholders that are, or at least should be, around the table in complex societal challenges. Such as overtourism, for example, which is a key issue in tourism. The Canvas even throws light on the stakeholders that are not around the table. Again, this is something that is all-too-often forgotten. So, what we see is that, in what is a very messy world, the Canvas really works. Similarly, in what is a very

messy social system, the Canvas provides guidance, at least for those who should be around the table. Who should say something. Who should engage, as well as when and where they should do so. This is how we used the Canvas. Literally bringing stakeholders together and getting them to talk to one another on the topics at hand. This was very evident, for example, at the city DNA conference in Hamburg last year, where Claudia and I facilitated a workshop. The discussions, which involved a limited diversity of stakeholders, were mainly themed on tourism. In our workshop, participants realised that they needed the involvement of different stakeholders. They identified different power relationships and it brought out into the open just how valuable it is to discuss these elements, which is something that happens too infrequently in tourism. There are, of course, dozens of other tools for other purposes/counts, but the great thing about the Canvas is that it can include them. Like the suggestions on the rear side of the Canvas cards, for example. One thing I had not even thought about before is that the Canvas explicates differences between concepts that seem similar. In this way, it forces you to make explicit or clarify what you mean, rather than talk about a challenge in a fuzzier or generalist narrative way that can mean different things to different people. For example, in design projects, design teams can sometimes mix up the common purpose, aspired impact and concrete results. These items are all different, but it is so easy to describe them all in a vague way. Either because of a lack of understanding of the topic, to avoid conflict, or even to hide potential issues. In the Canvas, the above-mentioned issues are deliberately separate cards that force you to be more explicit and to distinguish common purpose from impact and concrete results. Filling all these in can get confrontational, because it forces people to commit. And committing is something that is far-too-easy to avoid. Powerful stakeholders, in particular, have become very adept at not committing. This is not always a bad thing; after all, they do not necessarily have to. But it is useful to get the fact that they are not committing out in the open, and that is what happens when you use the Canvas. It is in cases like this that I see the great value that it adds. For tourism, it adds value in nearly every discussion on multi-stakeholder engagement relationships. The Canvas is a very useful tool if you are setting up a cooperation, or even if you are already in a cooperation. It helps address questions like: 'Why is this not working?' and 'Why are we not making progress?'. I also see the Canvas as a learning tool, because using it could surprise you. This is something we saw during the Hamburg conference. The workshop participants were not working together on an actual joint challenge. They were just a group of stakeholders from across Europe working on a more hypothetical issue in a workshop context. Yet just having them discuss the co-design elements through the cards made participants already realise what they were not doing right and what it was that they were missing. That is when you really start using the Canvas as a learning tool.

Wina
I hear you giving tips already. Claudia, for example, suggested that the Canvas is not self-explanatory at the moment, while Ko thinks it could be used for other topics. What kind of other topics do you have in mind Ko?

Ko
Given its flexibility, I wondered whether the Co Design Canvas could also be useful with a more limited number of stakeholders. The danger, of course, is trying to make it a Jack of all trades by using it for everything. I think you might be able to, provided you are a very good facilitator in social processes, but then you would be doing these things anyway, I assume. A good facilitator will put the focus on where he or she sees that the group needs to go. And, of course, the Canvas can support that. Having separate cards that support you in exploring only one element at a time will help. But if it concerns individual relationships between only two stakeholders, I think you might need something else. The Canvas was not designed for that. It is meant for larger groups, larger concepts and workshops. I am convinced that there are probably already very good ways and means of doing this and it would be very useful to integrate these in the overarching framework of the Canvas. In essence, the Canvas is a talking framework. That is its intrinsic value. It would be very interesting to see where you could go with it all. Perhaps, if people were to start experimenting with this Canvas and just take it into different places, they might completely rip it apart. Which would be fine. It would make for an interesting study.

Wina
And getting back to Claudia's self-explanatory issue, this is major research question. In what way does the Manual help with this? Or is there still something missing?

Claudia
I read the Manual. It is very rich, because it explains the co-design components and cards and, later on, explains the facilitation that Ko referred to earlier. If you read the whole Manual, it is quite clear what you can do with the Co-Design Canvas. However, the question is, will you really understand the whole tool by reading the Manual? Looking at Bloom's taxonomy taxonomy (Anderson et al., 2001), I learned that just understanding is not enough. To really take ownership, co-design needs to be personally experienced and applied. It takes immersion to deeply understand the Canvas and then apply it. People need more experience, like Ko said,

to know that it could be used in a specific scenario. That requires a deeper understanding. Like first analysing and then being able to apply it. I noticed this with the students too, which is why I set up workshop variations inspired by Bloom's taxonomy. Last year I adapted the Co-Design Canvas workshops with students from a more cognitive orientation to the experiential. I tried to focus on students in the development and design process and depending on their stakeholder knowledge, I started differently. I let novice students define relevant stakeholders and then asked them who they had not yet talked to or contacted? I let them circle those and only then did I introduce the Co-Design Canvas. Then, I explained that this canvas tool helps you think about relevant questions to ask stakeholders. So, in answer to your question, I see the Canvas as a modular toolkit that has all different cards and blocks that can be combined like Lego blocks in many different shapes, depending on the prevailing situation. It could be, for instance, that at the kick-off of a multi-stakeholder project, you focus mainly on the purpose for change, impact and concrete results. But it could also be applied differently; perhaps as a mid-term assessment to focus on the stakeholder part. I think what the Canvas might miss is a more fun, easy and flexible way of playing with it. Like with Lego blocks. I am thinking along the lines of developing a kind of an interactive flow game. When using it you find out the situation you are in, the role that you play, and the challenge that you face. It is like in a casino, where a one-armed bandit gives you three symbols demanding your attention. A serendipity plan, if you like. One that tells you to start with the purpose of change, impact and concrete results. This can be done at a basic or advanced level. Like a facilitation exercise. Or your own customised version of parts of the Co-Design Canvas. You can have your own rules, your own itinerary of a logical sequence for your specific needs in

a specific problematic situation. By then, we will already be combining it with what is very practical, like plug-and-play basically. I think we just prototyped a new concept, which I might use in the PhD that I am about to start.

Wina
Great, we will write a second book then.

Claudia
And maybe it will not be a book ☺

Ko
I think this would be fun! You could use these concepts in a simple, serious game which forces you to take on different roles, with the computer playing the roles of the others for you. That is when you would see different perspectives and you would have to address the same challenge from a different stakeholder perspective. That alone is already very useful in understanding what other stakeholders want or need to do, as well as what their aspirations are. The game could be just a simple 30-minute session in which you do not even need to have an understanding of the Canvas at all because it just provides the source in the background. You just play the game and gain some understanding. It would be much more limited, but different too. You would basically get a different kind of canvas but this could be a very interesting learning experience.

Claudia
You have hit on something interesting there, because nowadays there are so many opportunities to involve AI tools for exactly that type of roleplay. Supposing, for example, we are involved in a project in which a mayor is, for the sake of argument, a factual thinker. We could use the Crystal knows

plugin on Chrome where you open a LinkedIn profile and it gives you the probabilities of his/hers/its DISC personality, including custom communication scripts and the relevant do's and don'ts of this person. And while it would not be 100 per cent accurate, it would generate a highly probable DISC personality analysis of this person. You could use it to learn how to convince this very fact-based mayor. You then prompt Chat GPT with the personality information and adapt the temperature. Temperature controls the creativity or randomness level of output. A higher temperature (e.g., 0.7) results in more diverse and creative output, while a lower temperature (e.g., 0.2) makes the output more deterministic and focused. I would set a low temperature for accurate output. Now, imagine that you are in a collaboration with various stakeholders. You apply the Six Thinking Heads of Edward de Bono. You can experiment with different replies for the mayor for his/her/its purpose of change. That would represent a completely new dimension in applying AI in co-design processes, eventually roleplaying those who are not even there. Moreover, it could be interesting to involve non-human stakeholders, such as flora, fauna and future generations. We would then be stretching co-design processes beyond our own lifetime.

Ko

With regards to the nature, I agree that it is very useful to have that in the Canvas. But it is also useful to see if there is a way of addressing systemic change. At the moment, there is a risk that the Canvas will instigate and boost change, mostly within the current system, rather than breaking, or breaking out of, this system. Breaking out the system may be needed, however, to come to the transition that we argue is needed to overcome issues like climate change, or resilient and sustainable city systems. So, it would be interesting to also explore a more radical canvas that forces you to leave the current system. I think that this is the next step, because I wonder if the current canvas lives within the current system. The Canvas reveals the impatience of the current system, but is it meant to break that system? Once you start engaging with societal challenges like climate change, the refugee crisis as a consequence of climate change, the plastic crisis, or the fact that water is evaporating, the logic of the Canvas can be applied.

Wina
Is there anything I forgot to ask you about the Co-Design Canvas that you think is important?

Ko

Keep up the good work. Moreover, I would be interested to see how - like we have just discussed - the Canvas could be made more playful and systemic. I think the danger is that if people use it too rigidly and literally, it becomes mainly aimed at highly intellectual people. The Canvas will then be an intellectual tool. And that will not lead to change.

Claudia

It is important to ask the question: 'How do you want to experience a co-design process with this Co-Design Canvas?'. You could have three-game levels, for example: beginner, advanced and expert. The Canvas could then be a customised journey played out according to your own gameplan. Moreover, I would like to address the visibility of the Canvas. Wherever I go - like the destination management conference in Hamburg, for example - everyone is really interested in the Canvas and amazed that they did not even know about its existence and how much value it can add. At the moment, you need to be a pretty smart person to find it on Google, or lucky enough to read about it or hear from Wina or one of us. Ergo, its existence is hardly common knowledge. We should think big. I would really love to see this as the model for co-design, along the lines of the Business Model Canvas. Our canvas could be a movement driver to make complex projects more successful. Maybe, it could even become the new future of co-design?

> ### Wina
> *That is interesting. Do you think the Canvas - as a structure or a way of working - could replace a current change- or design-process?*

Ko

The Canvas could not replace a well-known process and I am not certain whether it should. I think it should be seen as another way of doing this kind of thing. All these different lines of thought may have value in certain circumstances and for certain types of questions. I am not a proponent of linear tools, for example, but they are sometimes useful. For some stakeholders, this linear structure is helpful because they might have more difficulty engaging with more fluid models as canvasses. I think, 'replace' however, is far too strong a word. It is more like another way of looking. But I do think that for the majority of real-world questions, it is a more value-added way of looking. What could be useful is an additional tool to apply before the Co-Design Canvas. A tool to help identify where a certain group is in its thinking, what they can do and where they can go. Then you can decide to either go for a more systemic linear listing or a fluid one.

Claudia

I think you have already guessed that I do not agree, because I see this as a potential marriage. Why not combine them and see the strength of both together. I recognise the value of Design Thinking and, semester after semester, I see that Design Thinking alone is not enough. Concepts always need to be implemented in order to enrich desirability with feasibility and viability, both in a technological and economic context. A concept can make sense, but it might not be a good fit with the organisation. And what value will it then add? Therefore, you always need to consider all three lenses of innovation. The Co-Design Canvas is extremely flexible, but I acknowledge that that flexibility could also be a weakness. Experienced facilitators will just find ways to adapt it. But less-experienced facilitators might find the Canvas more difficult and need more guidance. The value of Design Thinking lies in its checks. You first need to know what to test in order to know what to prototype. And to prototype it, you have to know what the target group aspires to, needs and wants. I would see it more as a merge. How they can enrich one another. Who knows, maybe then *Co-Design Doing* will be the future?

Bio Hilma van Slooten

Hilma is a senior marketing professional. After having worked in large corporate companies like Achmea, she took the plunge and became self-employed in 2015. Her work consists mainly of project management or marketing of social projects. Her special interest lies in the field of dementia, which started after both her parents were diagnosed with the illness. This frustrating period in her life inspired her to set up a website to help family members, especially their offspring, find ways to give dementia sufferers a better quality of life.

Bio Jeroen Spoelstra

Jeroen is a designer who focuses on life-centred design. He lives with his family in a tiny village in the Spanish Pyrenees. Jeroen runs three creative enterprises: Unbeaten Studio, the Life-Centered Design School and a mountain bike guiding company. He helps creative professionals transition from human-centred design to life-centred design. He also works on impactful design projects, one of which is the dementia challenge of Hilma. Life-centred design gives a voice in the design process to biological ecosystems and non-user communities that did not have one before. And, in a way, that also includes people with dementia and maybe even their offspring, who are excluded from healthcare support processes. That, in a nutshell, is his interest in Hilma's social enterprise. He wants to give these 'victims', or 'underdogs', a place in society.

The CO-DESIGN CANVAS in the dementia domain

> **Wina**
> *Could you both briefly explain what it is that you do?*

Hilma

I am a social entrepreneur and I want to make sure that informal caregivers know how to deal with their parents' dementia. My philosophy is that life does not end with a dementia diagnosis. With the right kind of help and support you can live at home for longer than you might think. Together with Jeroen, I have developed a platform comprising two things. The first of these we call the lifeline. It lists the steps you can take to cope with dementia. Most of the time, it is not clear to people what the next step is in the process and what you can pro-actively do to make life easier. The second is the regional offering. My website makes it easier for informal caretakers to find existing support opportunities and possibilities when caring for parents. I have based my concept on positive health philosophy, a concept of Machteld Huber. In addition to healthcare, the concept focuses strongly on quality of life and mental care. The emphasis lies on continuing to live at home. It is about very practical things, like how to deal with your household, administration, eating healthy, and so on. Or still being socially active with your partner, family or friends. Moreover, it shows the opportunities you still have during the later stages of dementia, such as 24-hour care. It makes the children of dementia sufferers better prepared for what is to come. People see and experience that my concept works. I use my professional marketing skills and personal experience to engage people and personal blogs to drive them to my platform and find the help they need. But people often seek this help when it is too late, usually waiting for a crisis situation before reaching out. I want this to happen sooner. The earlier you seek help for dementia, the more ways there are of dealing with it and the easier it can be. There are already too many crises, too many people not knowing what to do. It could be easier for them. There is plenty of supply to meet their demand, but at the moment there is little connection between the two.

Jeroen

I am a designer focusing on life-centred design and I live with my family in a tiny village in the Spanish Pyrenees. I have two design enterprises: Unbeaten Studio and the Life-Centered Design School. We help creative professionals transition from human-centred design to life-centred design. Next, we work on impactful design projects, and one of those is the challenge of Hilma. Life-centred design gives a voice to biological ecosystems and non-user communities that did not have a voice before in the design process. In a way that also refers to people with dementia or maybe even the children of people with dementia which are not included in healthcare support processes. That is kind of my own interest in the project of Hilma. I want to give these 'underdogs' in society a place.

> **Wina**
> *How did you find out about the Co-Design Canvas?*

Jeroen

I heard about it via your LinkedIn post.

Hilma

I listened to your inaugural speech on the web[4]. I was very intrigued about how you handle and look at problematic situations and collaborations. We got in touch and you offered to look at my challenge from a co-design perspective. Then, we decided to use the Canvas to explicate my challenge and together we then set up a grant application proposal for a design-research project.

> ### *Wina*
> ***And what was it about the Co-Design Canvas that appealed to you in the beginning?***

Hilma

It reminded me of the Business Model Canvas, which I use myself for other projects. The Canvas had a familiar look and feel about it. I like working in a condensed and structured manner. The Canvas helps me to see the whole picture, at a glance. That appealed to me. What I liked about the Canvas was that it brought me more than the Business Model Canvas, because it also includes the problematic context. I found it really fascinating to discuss all stakeholders' interests, knowledge and power. That, to me, was a big addition to what I already knew. The Canvas makes you go much deeper into the relationships between one another. Why you do the things you do. And getting to know from other parties why my platform appeals to them. Like yourself Wina. Your interest was spurred because, as an informal caretaker of your mother-in-law, you could identify with my challenge.

Jeroen

I was incredibly intrigued by the whole power thing. It is not something you generally think about in design. It adds a whole extra dimension to design, because no one ever, or hardly ever, talks about these things in my experience in design or co-design work. Like who is responsible for what? Who has the power to decide? Normally, in a design session anybody and everybody can just come up with a lot of interesting ideas. Afterwards, at the end of the session, people then go their own ways. But with the Co-Design Canvas you know who is involved and who can, and will, do what. That increases the success rate of design projects, as well as their outcomes and impact. That, in a nutshell, is one of the major aspects that intrigued me.

Hilma

I completely understand what you are saying. Most of the time, many ideas will be bandied about but there will be little clarity on who will implement them. But if you use the Co-Design Canvas before starting the ideas phase, I think it will stimulate commitment. You commit yourself to actually doing something. The Canvas almost serves as a social contract before you even start designing.

> ### *Wina*
> ***How would you describe or define the Co-Design Canvas to others?***

Jeroen

The Canvas is a tool that helps you get started with multiple actors in a very accountable way. 'We are going to do this together', as it were. The Canvas is a very deliberate co-design tool that helps you get started in a co-design process. It is indeed a social contract that commits to the fact that we will

---

4   www.youtube.com/watch?v=Aq5phD5jAts&t=1s

design something together. But, of course, it does not mean that you have to go through the whole process together. There are parts during which you might need to step out and someone else will step in, because it makes more sense at that moment. I think it is interesting that the three of us used the Canvas to start up our collaboration and set up a grant application. And further down the line, to start the design project, we will use it again because we will also need other stakeholders to get involved. Then, the Canvas can be used to explain where and how we started, to show the preparatory work that we did. And to explain that we now are moving on to the next phase. In other words, you can use the Canvas several times during a co-design process.

Wina
In what ways is the Co-Design Canvas important to your project, your work, your social company? Now or in the future?

Hilma
Well, as my company grows, not everybody will be on the same page. Therefore, I think the Canvas could help me start up collaborations with new people and new parties. The Canvas can even help elucidate matters, because what you have to do becomes clearer every time you discuss it. When you start collaborating with people, you can already say: 'This is the focus', 'This is where we are heading', and 'This is why we are doing it'. Then you can elicit input from the new stakeholders that you are working with. That could be of great help.

Jeroen
During a social design project, you are always on the lookout for new people to join in. The Co-design Canvas helps me to see if there is a good match, whether there is compatibility in terms of values, purpose and similarity in the results that we are aiming for. I think that is really helpful. When you look at the power thing, I am not only working with the underdogs in society, but also, for example, with nature. Working with the Canvas allows me to invite NGOs that protect a certain area and give them more power. Or at least talk about these power dynamics with the stakeholders. I think that is a really important aspect of the work that I do.

Wina
In what ways have you already used the Canvas?

Jeroen
We have organised co-design sessions around the Natura 2000 areas here in the Pyrenees and we invited all the stakeholders that have conflicting interests. Think about hunters and ecological farmers, for example. You know that they are opposites, they have different interests and perspectives. But by collaborating and talking about what are we going to do together, what issues are we going to work on in a co-design way, you avoid the 'I am for' and 'I am against' type of polarised discussions. The Canvas is not about disagreement, it makes it possible to bring to the table things that are important and relevant for every party. By literally giving the underdog stakeholders (which can be children of people with dementia or a glacial lake here in the Pyrenees) a voice in the process, I am giving them power.

Hilma
The three of us used the Canvas to plot the challenge that I faced of the offspring of people with dementia being too late in arranging care. We looked at all the different aspects, the context, the different parties involved in this challenge,

as well as the desired outcomes or wishes for the future. We used the Canvas to get more knowledge about the challenge at hand. We were very much into that, whereas normally what I do is much more about making things work and not going into so much depth. I realised that what I thought was a clear problem, was not really clear enough. We needed to dig a lot deeper into the challenge. But maybe we did so too much, because we kept going back and forth to elaborate on why these children do not seek help in time. I was seeking the solution and I hoped I would find it earlier. I got rather impatient. But I trusted your expertise as people and professionals. I have worked with Jeroen before. Together we laid the basis of the lifeline on the website themed on taking and keeping in control of dementia in 2019, something that still amazes and appeals to people. My personal blogs about my experiences with my parents with dementia seem to attract the necessary traffic and lead the children of people with dementia to the support they need for where they are in the dementia process. Together with you, I am now looking for drivers to motivate them to seek that support sooner.

Jeroen

Well, Hilma you were the initiative taker and the owner of the challenge from the start. By involving Wina and I, as well as other people, your challenge became a shared one. That is probably why you felt it was going back and forth a bit. Our process started with your problematic situation. However, the Canvas sessions showed me what my part in the challenge was.

Hilma

For me as a marketing person, co-design goes into much more depth on a personal level. I appreciate that, because I no longer believe in marketing as a selling concept or tool.

We now need solutions that really affect people on a personal level. The process might be tough, but at the end of the day we will get better results for those living with dementia. The old way of doing quantitative or qualitative research failed to generate the right solutions, so that is not the way. I was looking for another way. I did not know upfront whether we would end up with the right solutions, but it was well worth trying and I like experimenting.

Jeroen

Thanks for your trust. For me, design research is like learning: you put something out in the world, you get feedback and learn from it. Hilma might feel that we did not achieve a lot in a tangible sense, but we certainly did a lot of constructive research. As a new way of working, the Co-Design Canvas was probably more intuitive for me because I have been working in a co-design context for the past 20 years. What I appreciate now, after carrying out research in discussions with hundreds of designers for the past eighteen months, is that there are not enough tools like this one.

Wina

Do you think the Co-Design Canvas could replace a design- or a change-process?

Jeroen

I do not see the Canvas as a design-process replacement, but it could be seen it as a plug-in for a co-design process. As I mentioned earlier, the Canvas could be used in different phases of a design project, because it helps you reflect on the project and where you are at a certain moment. It also helps stakeholders to check that everyone is still aligned. To ask questions such as: 'Are we looking at the right thing?', 'Should we be broadening our scope?' 'Should we diverge, or is it time to narrow things down and converge?'. Here, I think, is where the Canvas is really useful. The Canvas is definitely helpful when it comes to aligning, as well as serving as a departure point for the next design phase. You could do the research part with parties X, Y and Z, for example, and the design part with parties A,B and C.

Wina
Do you have any tips that you would be willing to share?

Hilma
The Canvas should be the departure point for all collaborations. Instead of just getting together, looking at the problem and then suggesting all kinds of solutions, the Canvas gives you a better understanding of just who is at the table. This is particularly the case when it comes to debates on your expertise, what you bring to the table, what power you have, your ability to act, or not. I think that all this is very valuable.

Jeroen
Maybe it would be interesting to see at which point in the design process you would use the Canvas? And when do you feel that it is the right moment to use the Canvas? This is something that really interests me. You start a project with an initial research phase, exploring what the challenge is, then move on to establishing what you actually want to achieve. Perhaps I would be able to conduct the Canvas by myself first, then after the initial phase bring in the other stakeholders that I have in mind. Maybe, I could even use the Canvas as a selection tool. This is what I want. Do you fit in? I noticed after using the Canvas once in a life-centred design online course - that the Canvas should be a play between interconnected methods.

Hilma
I would like to add here that you then need people in the business who are into experimenting. It was difficult for me in the beginning to understand what we were doing. And because I had already done one design-research process with Jeroen, I knew it was going to be a lot of work, but that in the end it would turn out OK. For me, it is difficult, because in business you are used to going from B to C. For people other than designers and change makers, trust is then an important aspect. Moreover, it is key that participants are like-minded people who are into experimenting. When working with the Canvas, you have to get used to a different way of working.

Wina

For my last question I would like to ask if I forgot to ask you anything or if there is something else you would like to share?

Hilma

I would be interested to know how you distribute it, because I think the Canvas has huge potential in business as well as in governmental circles. I am very interested to see how you take it further. I would recommend it to other people, to other parties so to speak. The Canvas really has something to add and I hope you can make that clear to people.

Jeroen

Can we make a specific Co-Design Canvas that is really focused on nature and includes sustainability? That would be hugely interesting. How can we allow for the laws of nature, for example? And how can we allocate more power to nature?

Wina

Great! Let us make a sketch of this new so-called Eco-Design Canvas! I agree with the idea that stakeholders in the Canvas are not limited to just people. A stakeholder can be nature as well. For me, the Co-Design Canvas is not static; it is dynamic and I think everybody can work on it and with it. It can be changed as it is under Creative Commons.

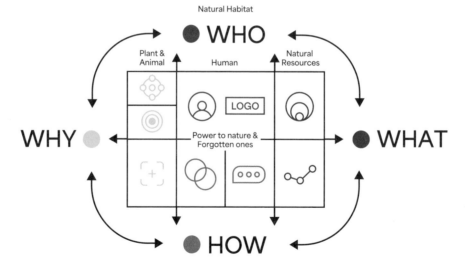

Figure 7: The why, how and what through eyes of all living.

" The Canvas gives everybody the space to bring in their own perspectives on sub-themes. "

" The Canvas helps you reflect on the initiative and project and where you are at a certain moment. "

" The Canvas helps me to see if there is a good match, whether there is compatibility in terms of values, purpose and similarity in the results that we are aiming for. "

" The Canvas almost serves as a social contract before you even start designing. "

" The Canvas gives everybody the space to bring in their own perspectives on sub-themes. "

" The Canvas increases the success rate of your design projects, as well as their outcomes and impact. "

The CO-DESIGN CANVAS for change makers

Wina
Wina
Given that you are not yet acquainted with one another, perhaps an introduction will be appreciated?

Frits

I work for Inholland University of Applied Sciences as a project portfolio manager and a team lead for programme managers. I use many tools and methodologies while working with colleagues in multi-disciplinary teams. One of those tools, which I experienced in our internal changemaker course, is the Co-Design Canvas. The Canvas is a great entry to starting-up a discussion about a subject. Not a specific problem, but a subject. And I stress subject here, because for me it is not a problem or a challenge but a social or digital development that makes me think about its implications. It demands that we think about it together, which stimulates us as stakeholders and makes us curious. It is adventurous and becomes a quest, which makes us insecure. Which is okay if we can do it all in a safe environment. That safe environment is created together at the beginning and you continue to invest in it during the process. The Co-Design Canvas process is about all the different perspectives. Most of the time I work on major change topics in which the digital component forms a big part. At the moment, for example, I am working together with several colleagues, with whom I am making iterations in developing a vision on a smart campus. It is a discussion about smart working. But what exactly is smart? I do not yet know whether the title is right, but that is the working title right now.

Josephine

At the moment, I am working an interim period in the Inholland University of Applied Sciences because of someone else who is on a maternity leave. For the time being, I am part of the domain on health, sports and social work. I head the policy department, which has about nine employees. We work on educational innovation and quality insurance. I became familiar with the Co-Design Canvas before this though. Back in January 2021, Wina presented the Co-Design Canvas in a digital version on MIRO at our Design Science Research group online meeting. And I was very taken by it. In 2022, I again encountered the Canvas when a colleague of Wina presented the big physical canvas carpet during our research and education day. When I and my colleague - the domain controller - René Zoon were assigned to renew the planning and control cycle for the domain, we wanted the whole team to be active with the new strategic themes. For that reason, during a two-day session with about 40 people, we used the Canvas to raise attention for strategic subjects and to form co-working groups.

Wina
What was it about the Canvas that appealed to you?

Frits

Well, it is always a struggle when you work with grand challenges and assignments to make change possible in an organisation. There are invariably different departure points. I am always very keen on establishing whether everybody is on the same information level. What usually happens in these sessions is that a few people will start assuming that everybody knows what they are talking about. I noticed that the Co-Design Canvas helps in this respect by slowly getting everybody reading from the same page. The Canvas gives everybody the space to bring in their own perspectives on sub-themes. In change processes, careful preparation is key. If you skimp on preparation you will slow progress down in the next phases. Normally, people get nervous when you talk about change. They want you to speed up, to see the opportunities ASAP and make sure that they are there in time. If you ask a lot of people to participate in such a change process, you must accept that it will start slowly because you will have to listen to the perspectives of all the participants in that process. If you do not listen to them, you will eventually slow the following phases down. Therefore, it is better to start slowly at the beginning of a change process then heed the other perspectives during the later stages.

Josephine

For me, it is also imperative to collect all those different elements before starting a joint enterprise. I really like the elements of the Co-Design Canvas. The Canvas forces you to think about the type of impact you want to make. It is also a tool in which you can place the subject at the centre, with the background of the teams as a kind of secondary layer. I find this interesting. As a change maker, I like to identify the people who are prepared to invest the effort in an intriguing topic: in forming the team. The central stakeholder card is very useful in collecting these insights before you start. It establishes who is in, who is not, what is their power, where they belong, and their interest in the subject. In my own session however, I might not have thought this through well enough before I started, because all types of managers seemed to have similar

interests. Frits, on the other hand, might have had a bigger number of employees with whom to use that specific element of the Co-Design Canvas. But it did not really work out for me. I can, however, identify with the gradual way of working, first collecting all those perspectives before you start running in a certain direction. After all, that direction might be the wrong one or you might be overlooking relevant alternatives

Frits

The way I look at co-design and the Co-Design Canvas is that in reality you have to deal with all kinds of stakeholders and their interests. Actually, as a change maker, I am not interested in stakeholders' positions in an organisation. I am interested in you, in the expertise that you can bring to the table. I do not really care where you are positioned in the organisation. With a change subject like the smart campus, I need experts at the table. If these experts are enthusiastic about the developments within the co-design process, they will talk about it to their directors, for example. And these directors will usually lean on the expertise of their experts and the director will give the go ahead. You have to start with a large group and you might end with a small team. But make sure that all the stakeholders are kept informed.

Josephine

Can I ask you a few questions, Frits? Was the group you worked with initially a bigger group than that you eventually started working with? Were you able to gather those different areas of expertise without focusing on their positions? And did you have a large variety of expertise in the group that you worked with?

Frits

I can only answer 'yes' to these questions.

Josephine

Maybe the difference was that I was not able to choose who joined the sessions. That was decided even before we chose to work with the Canvas. I like the idea of starting with a more bottom-up approach.

Frits

The subject or challenge of the strategic plan that you were addressing with the Co-Design Canvas was played out in a group of people within one domain. So their interest regarding the challenge was, in fact, very high. In such a situation you have to deal with all kinds of power elements within the team. My subject involved the whole Inholland organisation. That is when you see that when experts who are interested in the subject accept the invitation, they participate with a genuine motivation. For the next few years I have also been assigned to report on ISO management across all six Inholland locations. I have already conducted two sessions and the interesting thing is that I got the impression as a facilitator that we were eventually getting somewhere. However, when we were almost at the end of the second session, something came up. The initial question turned out not to be the right question. The right question was not 'How we will do the ISO management within the organization?', but "How do we get a position within the matrix organisation as ISO management team?" Will the team be acknowledged and recognised as a relevant stakeholder or discussion partner within the Inholland organisation? That is a totally different thing to do and out of the comfort zone of the team. But it needs to be explored first before we can really achieve anything.

Wina

What I think you both discuss here is the ability to motivate people and get them involved. What did using the Co-Design Canvas teach you about this?

Frits

What I am learning from the Canvas is that a co-design process is never finished. Everything you write or draw down in the boxes and cards of the Canvas is important. Everything is important. Period. And from a facilitator's point of view it is important to connect those different Canvas cards. Bring in the holistic view and keep on repeating it. This is because people tend to focus on one part and develop a tunnel vision. They need to be brought back to the total overview that the Canvas provides. That is also what I am training myself to do.

Josephine

I'm afraid we did not continue working on the Canvas long enough to reach that point. We only had 90 minutes, by which time we had only managed to fill in most of the elements and cards. Moreover, the facilitators only received 30-minutes' training on how to work with the Canvas, which, in hindsight, was also not ideal. We were very dependent on the different styles and qualities of the facilitators. But the Canvas provided a wonderful structure in stimulating a meaningful dialogue on our strategic topics. When I transcribed the summaries of the facilitators, I found that, for such a limited collaboration time, the stories that emerged from the Canvas sessions were very rich, structured and complete. It really struck me that the Canvas delivered an integral vision. Moreover, I also realised that some people are less supportive of design-based ways of working than I am. That is something to consider before.

Josephine only used the Co-Design Canvas once, in a workshop. What do you think would happen if we were to use the Canvas in the same way that we use change- or design-processes?

Frits

I do not think the Canvas can replace change- or design-processes. The Canvas is more like a tool or implement that you need in your toolbox as a change maker. As a professional, you need to know when you can take the Canvas out of your toolbox and when you can actually start using it. That is when it becomes a great way of working together. However, I am also reluctant to use the word 'tool'. The Canvas is a great way of working with different kinds of players to make sure that everybody is on the same page.

Josephine

In a real multi-stakeholder process, the worth of the Canvas lies in its ability to also see the system as a whole. It might then, for example, be used to measure the progress made by triple-helix, quadruple-helix or quintuple-helix collaborations. What could then be helpful is to develop 'indicators' to monitor the progress that is made in that multi-stakeholder group. There is also impact to consider, something that is difficult to measure. I think if you measure the progress made by the Canvas you will see all types of group-forming, -norming, and -storming. That is something I think you can measure with the Co-Design Canvas. Unfortunately, in my experience with it, we had insufficient time to learn about that. The Canvas can also be used in all types of other change processes. I am thinking here along the lines of the agile approach, for example, but then as just one of the steps. I favour an instrument that can be used once every six months,

for example, because then the Canvas might be used to document your process. The Canvas certainly has that potential.

Frits

You will use the Canvas to get people around the table to discuss the challenge. I worked for Novell for a few years, a big American software company. In their sales department, they always use the Miller Heiman sales methodology, with which you had to present to your fellow salespersons how well you know your customer, which in my case was KLM. I thought I knew my customers, but I got all red flags because; apparently, because I did not know them well enough. When you look at the Co-Design Canvas it is pretty much the same: how well do you know your co-workers? What are their interests? What expertise do they have? What are their competences? What competence do you need in the context of a challenge being tackled with the Co-Design Canvas?

Wina

Do you mean that the Co-Design Canvas could make people aware of how well they know their co-workers, or how well you know your fellow students or peers in a team?

Frits

You got it! But there is also the question of where can they find the Canvas. In this book, or a white paper or a podcast or on YouTube - whatever. You should make sure that people are aware of the existence of the Canvas and that it can be used in change processes. Maybe a gaming component in the Canvas would also be helpful?

Josephine

Currently, the Canvas is mainly used as a means or a way of working, but it would be stronger if you could say what the goal of the Canvas is. Maybe you are omitting to say this because it can be multiple things. Perhaps, as Frits says, you should create awareness by working with the Co-Design Canvas. But I think it would be helpful if there is a kind of obvious over-arching objective. This might then help you as a facilitator to select the Canvas as a tool. To find out if it is the best tool for the job in hand.

Wina
And finally, is there anything that you think I forgot to ask you?

Josephine

I am still a bit undecided. Perhaps that is the best word. Undecided about what the various impacts of using the Canvas are. Although it was not really my intention or initial objective for people to find one another, should that happen then I already have one box ticked. Now, I really support the idea of a follow up. I used it as a one-off at the moment, but I think repeating the Canvas, or parts of it, would be even more powerful. But we know that just one workshop never has lasting impact, right? Irrespective of which tool you use or work with. I really wonder how an ongoing, repeated reflection on the whole Canvas digitally on MIRO might support coming meetings and sessions.

Bio Marieke Zielhuis

Marieke works as a researcher with the Research Competence research group at the Utrecht University of Applied Sciences. She has a particular interest in the collaboration between research and practical partners. She is trained as an industrial design engineer, and has experience as project leader of design research projects. Since 2019, she has been doing her PhD project at Delft University of Technology. It focuses on the challenges that arise when developing knowledge for design practice within academic design-research projects.

Bio Koen van Turnhout

Koen works as a professor of Human Experience & Media Design, at HU University of Applied Sciences. He investigates the user experience of smart, data-driven products and services. The research questions he and his research group address include: How can machine intelligence be used to make digital products and services more enjoyable and better? What interaction qualities can be delivered through machine intelligence? And how does the context of interaction affect the user experience? Koen did his doctoral research in Industrial Design at the Eindhoven University of Technology, focusing on the use of voice interfaces in social contexts. Afterwards, he worked as a lecturer-researcher at the Arnhem and Nijmegen University of Applied Sciences, where he focused on the methodology and didactics of design research. Koen is a specialist in the field of human-computer interaction, design methods, and design research.

The CO-DESIGN CANVAS in design research

Wina
How did you find out about the Canvas?

Koen

You gave me your first prototype booklet of the Co-Design Canvas and I read through it. What is more, before this you had already explained to me how it came about. Later, as part of a plan we had to write an article about bridging the research-practice gap, we had a working session in which we discussed the Canvas as an intermediate-level knowledge product and the way that knowledge had been created in developing the Co-Design Canvas. This led to our Design Research Note article entitled: Towards a reciprocal flow of knowledge between practice and research: four perspectives on the research-practice gap.

Marieke

For me, it started by often hearing several colleagues mentioning the Canvas and hearing about the Canvas myself. Finally, I looked it up on the website to find out what it is all about. I suppose my introduction was gradually hearing more and more about it and realising that it was something I needed to take a look at. Later, as Koen mentioned, we started to work on our joint design research note.

Wina
And what was it about the Co-Design Canvas that appealed to you? Why did you feel the need to take a closer look?

Marieke

Firstly, I was curious why others were talking about the Canvas. It got me thinking that it might be useful in co-design processes. I found out that the Canvas has relevant co-design elements and seems doable at the same time.

Koen

The really neat thing about the Co-Design Canvas is that it is a successful attempt at bringing academic knowledge to a design process in a generative way. Researchers often say that if you follow guidelines X, Y and Z everything will go right, which is just like prescriptive knowledge. But this ignores the role of design itself, in which designers need to develop such prescriptions themselves. The Canvas is an excellent approach of activating people to design and improving their process without dictating what the outcome should be. Truth be told, it is actually quite rare for knowledge and research outcomes to have that quality.

Marieke

I agree. The Canvas shows that knowledge from research can be properly implemented in practice. The cards it uses are the essence of the knowledge gained from research. The Canvas has become really usable in a way that works in practice, yet still corresponds with what emanated from research. That is not just neat; it makes sense. Furthermore, in developing the Canvas you did not make just one translation, you really went through a co-design process in practice to make the Canvas work in the real world, while maintaining the connection to what you know from research.

Marieke

As a researcher, I look into how research outcomes pan out in practice. And the Co-Design Canvas is a great example from which we can learn. I have not yet used the Canvas myself, but it could certainly be useful because all the relevant co-design aspects have been integrated into it.

Koen

I have the same two layers of interest. The first of these layers is a knowledge or theoretical view on the Canvas. How does this work? Why does it work? What are the properties of a canvas as a category of knowledge products? What are its similarities with the Business Model Canvas and where is that successful? How does that translate to this situation? Then, of course, I conduct co-design projects myself, so I could choose the Co-Design Canvas as a tool. But I have not used the Canvas yet. And the main reason for this is that, generally speaking, we do not conduct user-initiated designs. Usually, we do designs, because we feel something new is needed to pull people in. That is therefore not really participatory in the way the Canvas supports design. I am waiting for an opportunity to use the Canvas in a more bottom-up type of situation.

Wina

That is interesting. I have been using the Canvas to set up coalitions for new design-research projects.

Koen

If I were to use the Canvas to set up a new research project, I would expect it to bring structure, because it lists all the elements that you should be discussing in co-design and how they are connected. I also think that the Canvas will bring peace of mind, in the sense that holding a discussion without such a tool would allow people to react more to relationships, egos, trivialities and the like. Without the Canvas everybody pushes their own agenda; with it you get a much more cooperative attitude.

Marieke

I am considering using the Canvas in one of the research projects that I am supposed to start soon. In this project, we are supposed to co-design, but there are already a lot of boundaries. I would like to bring the Canvas in, because I want to open up the co-design process. Yet at the same time, I am also afraid that using it might lead to reactions such as: 'We do not want to discuss that now'. To many people, discussing these things is like opening Pandora's box. It is all about power. As researchers, we already set all the boundaries and we have decided to co-design within these confines. I am curious what would happen if we were to use the Canvas. I am also curious whether the researchers want to be really democratic. Although I am not so sure about that either. The Canvas could be a nice way of firing up the discussion among researchers. It could be an interesting experiment.

Koen

This is a whole new research topic about whether and how the Canvas can get rid of taboos in conversations. Not wanting to say something, or being reluctant to show vulnerability is one of the hardest things to overcome, right? I would assume that there are not many people, well nobody probably, who want to risk being explicit. Few people would be willing to put their head on the block, so to speak.

Wina

Neither of you has ever used the Co-Design Canvas, yet you are already elaborating on the fact that you might well do so. In what kind of context would you use it? And with which people or stakeholders?

Koen

If we take an imaginary case of starting a research consortium and using the Canvas in a research-grant proposal in which the stakeholders are partners from the real world, we could use it to figure out how to approach the research together. Actually, it might also be the case that citizens also need to be involved in drawing up the proposal, although we would normally not do that. One of the things we would need to discuss is just who will participate in the initial drawing up of the proposal. In other contexts, such as innovation in the medical field, you have innovation managers, healthcare workers, patients and designers. They would need to get together. So, we could use the stakeholder card. With a mixed group of stakeholders, I think the Canvas could be a very good departure point in conceiving how to approach a project. Thinking out loud here, most of the time we researchers identify stakeholders and write idealistic sentences about how they need to be involved and the important role that they play. But do we really practice what we preach? While thinking about stakeholders, you sort of recognise this mismatch immediately. It is important to decide which stakeholders should join in, and in which roles.

Wina

Exactly, and we should also think along the lines of individuals versus organisations. How do you think the Co-Design Canvas might help other researchers?

Koen

We are currently working on a concrete project in which we are not using the Canvas. This project is about second language acquisition, and it was initiated by healthcare professionals. Teaching a language is mostly done on a voluntary basis and these volunteers do not really have the knowledge to teach it properly, whereas speech therapists do have this knowledge, but cannot be paid for giving language lessons in the Dutch system. In this extensive co-design project, we are including all stakeholders and holding creative sessions to better understand how we can change the situation. The envisioned outcome and scope is a learning environment. We are participating in the project to facilitate the co-design process and only bringing in our standard design repertoire. We do wall sessions, cultural probes, the whole configuration field toolbox. In this case, the Canvas could have served as a first step for researchers in the conception of the project. I think the Canvas is the type of tool to use very early on in such a project. It could be used as a lens to ascertain whether our repertoire is configured correctly. But we are doing just fine in this language-acquisition project, so there is no pressing need to use the Canvas in it. That said, I am quite sure that the Canvas would have helped researchers feel less lost in how they approached this co-design process at the beginning. The Canvas would have supported them until they - at some point - stepped back and reflected on the research plan while executing it. My researchers are now executing and following the plan that I wrote. They are doing their best, but they do not have the strategic insight into why they are doing it this way. That is my responsibility as a professor. Had they used the Canvas, they would have had a lightweight way of applying that strategic lens. I think it would also have enabled them to configure what they are doing in a more effective way.

Wina
I hear you when you say that this project is running well. But supposing that was not the case, do you think the Canvas could be used as an evaluation or a reflection-in-action tool?

Koen
You make me think of a project in which we were designing digital health interventions on a municipality level with civilian initiatives. We worked in a participatory manner and at some point along the way there was a sort of a change. Whereas at the beginning we all wanted to learn from one another and talked in terms of 'we', later on the people we worked with said: 'We hired you to do the job, where is your knowledge?'. At some point, we started to make decisions for them. Then they flipped and contested our decisions because: 'You wanted to work in a participatory manner'. So what exactly was happening here? We were, in fact, involved in a power struggle throughout the whole project. The Canvas might have alleviated that power struggle. Or we could have at least used the Canvas as a form of repair tool. To repair the relationships, insist that we all co-design the research approach and ask questions like: 'Where do you want us to be experts?', 'Where are you the experts?', 'Where do you want us to be learners?'. Had we done so, they would have probably come up with more or less the same process that we were conducting, but then they or we all would have had ownership of that joint process.

Marieke
I would reach out to the Canvas when the need arises, so to speak. There would have to be an actual issue or emergency on the table. Especially, when there are power issues at play, the Canvas could function as a tool to facilitate the conversation. The type of emergency that would necessitate working with the Canvas could be conflicting goals, for example. That situation also readily relates to power, because more value is placed on some people's voices and objectives than it is on other people's. This is a disconnection issue. I see the Canvas as a tool that can provide something that you really need. I wonder if the Canvas is always used because you have this need, or whether it can also be used to plan something.

Koen
I think a key quality of the Canvas is that it creates an external safe space to have the discussion - away from the current structure. Using the Canvas encourages you to enter into a certain type of discussion dialogue. And discussing certain types of elements momentarily takes stakeholders out of their normal way of thinking. It creates a constructive setting. I think emergency cases are a very interesting possibility, but so too is the planning case, which is partly why it was designed.

Marieke
I would like to add to that. I need the Canvas now in an emergency case. And as I acquire more experience using the Canvas and perhaps enter a new trajectory in which I will need to plan ahead, I will again turn to the Canvas. That is how it would work for me. With that kind of experience behind me, I will be able to start planning new things. That is when you will be able to say: 'Wait a minute, this might happen; I can respond to that'. But first I need experience with the Canvas now, so that I can exploit its potential later.

Wina
I was wondering whether you think the Co-Design Canvas could replace current change- or design-process structures?

Marieke

No, I think the Canvas adds a new lens. This lens shows the different aspects of the co-design process that you need to consider. The other processes have different focuses. I think you could combine the Canvas with other processes. Having said that, I imagine that students might wonder which process they should use. And how exactly they will work together, which might confuse them. I think with students you could work with one of them. In reality, they could be combined.

Koen

The Canvas provides different attention points. I am thinking here of the community centred design process by Jennifer Preece, who basically took the human-centred design process and then set it in a community design setting. Community designers need to work on all aspects of human-centred design at the same time. So rather instead of phases, they need to see different aspects of the design as a stage (as in a podium). Basically, designers say: 'Sometimes you are here, other times you are there' and it is somewhat random where you are. And then you make switches, such as in the reflective transformative design proces.

I can imagine that the Co-Design Canvas could be a way of making those switches clear for design novices and junior designers and students. That you explain that the Canvas cards are attention points in co-design. Then, every day, or every week, the students can opt to focus on one or two main cards within the Canvas and then take their project further.

The next day, or the next week, they can then opt for yet another card. In this way, they can take the project closer and closer to its conclusion. What you then have is different stages at which you can act during the co-design process. That would be an excellent way of thinking to convey the essence of the Canvas to students. The big advantage of Design Thinking or the Double Diamond approach is that novices can plan the project from beginning to end. First we do this, and then we do that. That is why these processes do not really do a lot for an experienced designer. In my opinion, Design Thinking and Double Diamond processes are very generic and are far removed from the actual creative act of design. That said, they do provide a good departure point, in the form of a playbook on how you can reach the end of the project. The Canvas does not have that playbook yet. But if you could define routes how to go through the Canvas in time, it might be possible to use it in that way.

Wina
I was triggered when Marieke said that acquiring more experience with the Canvas will probably enable you to exploit its potential and translate it more freely. Where I think the Canvas might differ from current processes is that it is less linear. There are more routes through the Canvas that will take you to the outcome and impact that you are working towards. But do you think it might be too prescriptive, because you have to go through all the cards, while you can do that in every phase of a design process and in any order?

Koen

You do not have to be prescriptive, you could also give examples of how to do it. You could, perhaps, formulate possible routes and decision rules. Specifying in a particular process or project that we will use the eight cards in a particular order. You might visit these cards twice and then decide on the next card on which you will do an iteration in. What you then basically get is an agile process. First a sprint, at the end of which there is an evaluation, before deciding on the priorities for the next sprint. That is basically the structure you will use and this will help people pinpoint what is most urgent. That is something experienced designers are very good at, while novices will not yet know where to go and what to decide.

Marieke

As long as you are giving clear guidance on how to decide, novices can also make co-design decisions.

Koen

This is also the case with the project that I just talked about, the one about learning a second language. I just drew from the methodological repertoire that I have built up over the course of ten years. "If this is the challenge, we will need to configure the process like this". In a way, I do not even know what expertise I am putting on the table. Moreover, making all these implicit decisions involves a great deal of intuition. If you are a novice, you will not have the experience to make such decisions. Therefore, we need to make these decisions more explicit and more novice-proof.

Marieke

In taking the Canvas further, it would be nice to bear the interests of both novices and students, as well as experienced designers, in mind. Sometimes, a tool is only developed for a student audience. The same tool will not always work as well for more experienced professionals. In my opinion, we will have to keep both groups in mind.

Wina

Do you have any more tips or tricks as to how we could improve the Co Design Canvas?

Koen

I like Marieke's suggestion that the Canvas explanation could have a layered approach. Like an advent calendar, for example, in which you say that this is your level in co-design and then you use the Canvas in this way. At that point, you could stack approaches within the Canvas. That would be a very interesting approach. You start off with novices and then build up expertise. As a thinking frame you could even use the levels of expertise of Dorst & Lawson (2013), who provides general stages of design expertise. They explain the main things of concern on a beginner's level, on an intermediate level, and on an expert level. While you are an expert, you are actually creating the Canvas yourself and a vision through it. Then you can show how the Canvas changes across those stages/levels. That would be a very interesting research exercise.

Wina

Is there anything I forgot to ask you about the Canvas, or something that might be important for me to know?

Koen

The Canvas is a very nice piece of work and you did a great job. There is something very reassuring about it and I like the way it came about. The Canvas development trajectory is a perfect example of how you could approach the research-practice gap. In many ways, I myself am sometimes hindered by an expert mindset. Then, as a design researcher, I tend to think: 'let us make this tool for practitioners'. More often than not, we researchers think that others in the real world need a particular tool, so we develop it and for that, of course, we use participant input. If participants who are using the tool are very enthusiastic, everyone is happy, right? But when it just floats aimlessly in the practical environment, researchers will sometimes notice that their designs are not being used, or they are not getting feedback that it is being used, either in classrooms or elsewhere. That can partly be because of the push character of a research project. However, in developing the Canvas, you really used a co-creative approach in making it. This is a recursive thing, which is both nice and a best practice. To figure out along the way what support is needed, let it emerge in the project and then see how you can generalise that from there. That is a more abductive way of reaching out to the practical environment.

Marieke

If I might add, it struck me that you talk about the Canvas as a boundary object and an intermediate-level knowledge product. As such, it is also very much tied to you, Wina, acting as the boundary-crosser in this whole process. You are inhabiting both worlds and developed something that is congruent with the practical environment. I think this is actually what makes it work in practice.

" The Canvas helps by slowly getting everybody reading from the same page. "

FOCUS

Ongeving

De co-design focus geeft de samenwerking nog meer richting door het gezamenlijke veranderdoel in een bepaalde situatie met bepaalde betrokkenen te vertalen naar (een) concrete HOE KUNNEN WE-vraag/vragen.

> Waar moeten we ons nu echt op richten om de gewenste impact en concrete resultaten te kunnen bereiken? zodanig dat we … bereiken?
> Hoe kunnen we samen over wie wat gaat doen om resultaten en impact te bereiken?
> Hoe beslissen we … echt op richten om de gewenste impact en concrete resultaten te bereiken?

Epilogue

As Frits mentioned earlier, a collaborative and creative process for a societal challenge is *never finished*. And that also goes for the Co-Design Canvas as a tool for societal impact. And it is why I fully expect it to evolve.

The current co-design decision elements of the Canvas help people and stakeholders to get aligned and to collectively define the steps they will need to take in their own co-design process, which is something that both Koen and Gène stressed. It provides a structure, or framework, that things can fall into according to Anja. As all the interviewees implied, when combined with other change processes and the available design repertoire, the Canvas can be really supportive in setting up stakeholder coalitions that need to work towards a joint purpose. Many of the interviewees insisted that you have to experience the Canvas to appreciate its value. But for novices, such as students for example, the Canvas is not self-explanatory, as Koen and Claudia conceded. But on the plus side, people are used to canvas thinking as Hilma argued, which makes the Co-Design Canvas a much easier place to step into. And Gène, Claudia and Koen hit the nail squarely on the head when they said that routes or pathways through it for novices, advanced and expert co-designers would be very helpful. See Figure 8.

If you have already experienced the Canvas and perhaps even used it a few times, you will already be internalising the associated thinking, doing and feeling, as Gène and Marieke pointed out. The methodology, so to speak. That is when using the constituents of the Canvas will become less regimented and you will find yourself using it more flexibly, intuitively and situationally. Although the Canvas will place the focus on tackling challenges together, it will never solve all the social contingencies, problems and issues that are part and parcel of working together in the processes of change-making, transition or transformation. That said, it can, like Josephine intimated, pave the way for a more transparent group-forming, -norming and -storming. And to new idea directions.

With the earlier interviews, we gave a few illustrative journeys that show how, and in which domain and for what challenge or purposes, the Canvas has already been used. During the next few years we - my colleagues and I in the Societal Impact Design research group of the Creative Business Research Centre at the Inholland University of Applied Sciences - will be using the Canvas on some very interesting challenges in education, research and practice. One of these will be the question of sustainable farm takeovers, in which the Canvas will bring all sorts of stakeholders to the table, like policymakers, and future and past generations in farming. Moreover, we will expand the Co-Design Canvas thinking and use the Canvas more systemically and playfully, in line with the suggestions put forward by Claudia and Ko. And I can't wait for Jeroen to explore an Eco-Design Canvas in implementing the life centred perspective. Lastly, I hope – as Claudia and Gène reflected on – that this book will help spread the word and fuel the growth of a Co-Design Canvas community or movement in Co-Design Doing!

Acknowledgements

First, I would like to thank all the citizens and policymakers we worked with and the design museum project coordinator Anja Köppchen and strategist Gène Bertrand for their trust in the process, sharing their experiences and giving honest reflections on the processes to support the development of the Co-Design Canvas. Without them, the Canvas would not have come into being. Moreover, I would like to thank all users of the Canvas and especially the interviewees Koen, Claudia, Marieke, Ko, Hilma, Jeroen, Frits and Josephine for their time and honest reflections.

This work was supported by the European Union's Horizon 2020 Research and Innovation program under grant agreement No. 788217.

About the author

Wina Smeenk

Since 2021, Wina Smeenk is appointed as a Professor in Societal Impact Design at Inholland University of Applied Sciences. She is also both founder and chair of the Expertisenetwork Systemic Co-design (ESC) - a network of four universities of applied sciences in the Netherlands. Next, Wina is lab lead for the Inholland Urban Leisure and Tourism Lab in Amsterdam. In 2010 Wina launched her own empathic co-design agency 'Wiens Ontwerperschap'. She graduated from Delft University of Technology, where she studied Industrial Design, after which she spend over 25 years working as a strategist, co-designer and researcher for a variety of international businesses, government and non-profit organisations in many different product and service sectors. Moreover, she helped to develop innovative design-oriented educational programs. These include universities of applied sciences such as Inholland, the HAN and the HvA, as well as the VU, THNK, the Amsterdam School of Creative Leadership and the Faculty of Industrial Design at Eindhoven University of Technology. In 2019, she defended her PhD thesis '*Navigating Empathy, empathic formation in co-design processes*'. Wina has written several academic articles and she co-authored the book 'Design, Play, Change, a Playful introduction to Design Thinking', which was published by BIS in 2022.

References

- Cockton, G. (2013, June). *Design isn't a shape and it hasn't got a centre: thinking BIG about post-centric interaction design.* Proceedings of the International Conference on Multimedia, Interaction, Design and Innovation, 1-16.

- Dorst, K. (2010). *The nature of design thinking.* DTRS8 Interpreting Design Thinking: Design Thinking Research Symposium Proceedings, Pp.131-1391. DAB Documents.

- Fulton Suri, J. (2003). *Empathic design: Informed and inspired by other people's experience.* Empathic design: User experience in product design, Pp.51-58.

- Gudde, R. (2016). *Het agoramodel. De wereld is eenvoudiger dan je denkt.* ISVW Uitgevers, Leusden.

- Hess, J. L, & Fila, N. D. (2016). *The manifestation of empathy within design: Findings from a service-learning course.* CoDesign, 12(Pp.1-2), Pp.93-111. doi:10.1080/15710882.2015.1135243.

- Hummels, C., & Frens, J. (2009). *The reflective transformative design process.* In CHI'09 Extended Abstracts on Human Factors in Computing Systems, Pp.2655-2658.

- Kleinsmann, M., & Valkenburg, R. (2008). *Barriers and enablers for creating shared understanding in co-design projects.* Design studies, 29(4), Pp.369-386.

- Koskinen, I., Battarbee, K., & Mattelmaki, T. (2003). *Empathic design.* IT press.

- Kouprie, M., & Sleeswijk Visser, F. (2009). *A framework for empathy in design: Stepping into and out of the user's life.* Journal of Engineering Design, 20(5), Pp.437-448. doi:10.1080/09544820902875033

- Lawson, B., & Dorst, K. (2013). *Design expertise.* Routledge.

- Lee, J.J., Jaatinen, M., Salmi, A., Mattelmäki, T., Smeds, R., & Holopainen, M. (2018). *Design choices framework for co-creation projects.* International Journal of Design, 12(2), Pp.15-31.

- Meadows, D. (1999). *Leverage points.* Places to Intervene in a System.

- Milano, C. & Koens, K. (2021) *The paradox of tourism extremes. Excesses and restraints in times of COVID-19.* Current Issues in Tourism, published online, Pp.1-13.

- Osterwalder, A., & Pigneur, Y. (2010). *Business model generation: A handbook for visionaries, game changers, and challengers.* John Wiley & Sons Inc.

- Rotmans, J. & Loorbach D. (2009). *Complexity and transition management.* Journal of industrial ecology, 13(2), Pp.184-196.

- Plattner H. Meinel C. & Leifer L. J. (2011). *Design thinking: understand, improve, apply.* Springer.

- Sanders, E. B. N., & Stappers, P. J. (2008). *Co-creation and the new landscapes of design.* CoDesign, 4(1), Pp.5-18. doi:10.1080/15710880701875068.

- Sanoff, H. (1990). *Participatory Design: Theory & Techniques.* Raleigh, N.C: Bookmasters

- Simon, H. A. (1996). *The sciences of the artificial* (3rd ed.). Cambridge, MA: MIT Press.

- Smeenk, W. (2019). *Navigating empathy: empathic formation in co-design.* (Doctoral dissertation). Technische Universiteit Eindhoven.

- Smeenk, W., Köppchen, A., Bertrand, G. (2021). *The co-design canvas.* Link: www.siscodeproject.eu/labarticle/cubes-co-design-canvas-a-one-page-tool-for-social-change/ and www.inholland.nl/onderzoek/publicaties/the-co-design-canvas/

- Smeenk, W. & Willenborg, A. (2022). *Design, Play, Change. A playful introduction to designthinking.* BIS Publishers, Amsterdam.

- Smeenk, W. (2023). *Empathic co-design canvas: A tool for supporting multistakeholder co-design processes.* International Journal of Design.

- Smeenk, W., Zielhuis, M. & Van Turnhout, K. (2023) *Understanding the research practice gap in design research: a comparison of four perspectives.* Design Studies.

- Stappers, P. J. (2021). *Map of Systems Thinking in Science, Engineering, and Design.* Link www.studiolab.ide.tudelft.nl/studiolab/mapofsystems/files/2021/08/SystemsForScreen.pdf

- Van Turnhout, K., Andriessen, D., Cremers, P.H.M. (Eds), (2023). *Handboek Ontwerpgericht Wetenschappelijk Onderzoek.* Boom Uitgevers. Pp.23-37.

- Van Turnhout, K., Jeurens, J., & Bakker, R. (2015). Co-designing The Participation Ecology. In 4th Participatory Innovation Conference 2015, Pp.258.

- Woolrych, A., Hornbæk, K., Frøkjær, E., & Cockton, G. (2011). *Ingredients and meals rather than recipes: A proposal for research that does not treat usability evaluation methods as indivisible wholes.* International Journal of Human-Computer Interaction, *27*(10), 940-970. doi:10.1080/10447318.2011.555314.

Weblinks

Various design tools

www.bispublishers.com/design-play-change.html
www.toolkits.dss.cloud/design/method-card/empathy-map-2
www.toolkits.dss.cloud/design/method-card/wwwwwh-2
www.thepartneringinitiative.org/wp-content/uploads/2014/08/
Partnering-Toolbook-en-20113.pdf
www.nesta.org.uk/toolkit/diy-toolkit
www.dschool.stanford.edu/resources/design-thinking-bootleg
www.dschool.stanford.edu/resources/dschool-starter-kit
www.crystalknows.com
www.crystalknows.com/disc/types
www.debonogroup.com/services/core-programs/six-thinking-hats/
wwwdesignthinking.ideo.com

Inholland

www.inholland.nl/onderzoek/publicaties/the-co-design-canvas
www.inholland.nl/onderzoek/publicaties/design-play-change
www.inholland.nl/onderzoek/lectoraten/societal-impact-design
www.systemiccodesign.com
www.systemischcodesign.nl
www.ensut.eu
www.tourismlabamsterdam.nl
www.tourismlabrotterdam.nl

SISCODE

www.siscodeproject.eu/wp-content/uploads/2019/09/
toolkit-27092019-1.pdf
www.siscodeproject.eu/resources
www.siscodeproject.eu/repository
www.siscodeproject.eu/repository/wp-content/uploads/2020/04/
people-and-connection-map.pdf
www.siscodeproject.eu/repository/wp-content/uploads/2020/04/
stakeholders-map.pdf

Interviewees

www.regieopdementie.nl
www.unbeatenstudio.com
www.lifecentereddesign.school
www.instagram.com/lcd.school
www.dsr-group.nl

Inholland web

Colophon

Author - Wina Smeenk
Graphic design – Studio idiotēs & Daniël Maarleveld
Illustrations – Daniël Maarleveld & Floor de Jong
Photos - Claudia Mayer, Wina Smeenk, Studio idiotēs

Creative Commons 2023
BIS Publishers
Borneostraat 80-A
1094 CP Amsterdam
The Netherlands
T +31 (0)20 515 02 30
bis@bispublishers.com
www.bispublishers.com

ISBN 978 90 636 9678 8

  **B/SPUBLISHERS**